A LECTURE

ON

THE STUDY OF HISTORY

DELIVERED AT CAMBRIDGE,
JUNE 11, 1895

BY

LORD ACTON

LL D , D C L

REGIUS PROFESSOR OF MODERN HISTORY

WIPF & STOCK · Eugene, Oregon

Wipf and Stock Publishers
199 W 8th Ave, Suite 3
Eugene, OR 97401

A Lecture on the Study of History
Delivered at Cambridge, June 11, 1895
By Acton,
Softcover ISBN-13: 978-1-6667-3449-2
Hardcover ISBN-13: 978-1-6667-9039-9
eBook ISBN-13: 978-1-6667-9040-5
Publication date 8/25/2021
Previously published by Macmillan and Co., 1896

This edition is a scanned facsimile of
the original edition published in 1896.

Fellow Students,

I LOOK back to-day to a time before the middle of the century, when I was reading at Edinburgh, and fervently wishing to come to this University. At three colleges I applied for admission, and, as things then were, I was refused by all. Here, from the first, I vainly fixed my hopes, and here, in a happier hour, after five-and-forty years, they are at last fulfilled.

I desire first to speak to you of that which I may reasonably call the Unity of Modern History, as an easy approach to questions necessary to be met on the threshold by any one occupying this place, which my predecessor has made so formidable to me by the reflected lustre of his name.

You have often heard it said that Modern History is a subject to which neither beginning nor end can be assigned. No beginning, because the dense web of the fortunes of man is woven without a void ; because, in society as in nature, the structure is continuous, and we can trace things back uninterruptedly, until we dimly descry the Declaration of Independence in the forests of Germany. No end, because, on the same principle, history made and history making are scientifically inseparable and separately unmeaning.

" Politics," said Sir John Seeley, " are vulgar when they are not liberalised by history, and history fades into mere literature when it loses sight of its relation to practical politics." Everybody perceives the sense in which this is true. For the science of politics is the one science that is deposited by the stream of history, like grains of gold in the sand of a river ; and the knowledge of the past, the record of truths revealed by experience, is eminently practical, as an instrument of action, and a power that goes to the making of the future.[1] In France, such is the weight attached to the study of our own time, that there is an appointed course of contemporary history, with appropriate text-books.[2] That is a chair which, in the progressive division of labour by which both science and government prosper,[3] may some day be founded in this country. Meantime, we do well to acknowledge the points at which the two epochs diverge. For the contemporary differs from the modern in this, that many of its facts cannot by us be definitely ascertained. The living do not give up their secrets with the candour of the dead ; one key is always excepted, and a generation passes before we can ensure accuracy. Common report and outward seeming are bad copies of the reality, as the initiated know it. Even of a thing so memorable as the war of 1870, the true cause is still obscure ; much that we believed has been scattered to the winds in the last six months, and further revelations by important witnesses are about to appear. The use of history turns far more on certainty than on abundance of acquired information.

Beyond the question of certainty is the

question of detachment. The process by which principles are discovered and appropriated is other than that by which, in practice, they are applied; and our most sacred and disinterested convictions ought to take shape in the tranquil regions of the air, above the tumult and the tempest of active life.[4] For a man is justly despised who has one opinion in history and another in politics, one for abroad and another at home, one for opposition and another for office. History compels us to fasten on abiding issues, and rescues us from the temporary and transient. Politics and history are interwoven, but are not commensurate. Ours is a domain that reaches farther than affairs of state, and is not subject to the jurisdiction of governments. It is our function to keep in view and to command the movement of ideas, which are not the effect but the cause of public events;[5] and even to allow some priority to ecclesiastical history over civil, since, by reason of the graver issues concerned, and the vital consequences of error, it opened the way in research, and was the first to be treated by close reasoners and scholars of the higher rank.[6]

In the same manner, there is wisdom and depth in the philosophy which always considers the origin and the germ, and glories in history as one consistent epic.[7] Yet every student ought to know that mastery is acquired by resolved limitation. And confusion ensues from the theory of Montesquieu and of his school, who, adapting the same term to things unlike, insist that freedom is the primitive condition of the race from which we are sprung.[8] If we are to account mind not matter, ideas not force, the spiritual property that gives dignity, and grace, and intellectual value to history, and its action on the ascending life of man, then we shall not be prone to explain the universal by the national, and civilisation by custom.[9] A speech of Antigone, a single sentence of Socrates, a few lines that were inscribed on an Indian rock before the Second Punic War, the footsteps of a silent yet prophetic people who dwelt by the Dead Sea, and perished in the fall of Jerusalem, come nearer to our lives than the ancestral wisdom of barbarians who fed their swine on the Hercynian acorns.

For our present purpose, then, I describe as modern history that which begins four hundred years ago, which is marked off by an evident and intelligible line from the time immediately preceding, and displays in its course specific and distinctive characteristics of its own.[10] The modern age did not proceed from the mediæval by normal succession, with outward tokens of legitimate descent. Unheralded, it founded a new order of things, under a law of innovation, sapping the ancient reign of continuity. In those days Columbus subverted the notions of the world, and reversed the conditions of production, wealth and power ; in those days, Machiavelli released government from the restraint of law ; Erasmus diverted the current of ancient learning from profane into Christian channels ; Luther broke the chain of authority and tradition at the strongest link ; and Copernicus erected an invincible power that set for ever the mark of progress upon the time that was to

come. There is the same unbound originality and disregard for inherited sanctions
in the rare philosophers as in the discovery
of Divine Right, and the intruding Im-
perialism of Rome. The like effects are
visible everywhere, and one generation
beheld them all. It was an awakening of
new life ; the world revolved in a different
orbit, determined by influences unknown
before. After many ages persuaded of
the headlong decline and impending dis-
solution of society,[11] and governed by usage
and the will of masters who were in their
graves, the sixteenth century went forth
armed for untried experience, and ready
to watch with hopefulness a prospect of
incalculable change.

That forward movement divides it
broadly from the older world ; and the
unity of the new is manifest in the uni-

versal spirit of investigation and discovery
which did not cease to operate, and with-
stood the recurring efforts of reaction,
until, by the advent of the reign of general
ideas which we call the Revolution, it at
length prevailed.[12]   This successive de-
liverance and gradual passage, for good
and evil, from subordination to independence is a phenomenon of primary
import to us, because historical science has
been one of its instruments.[13]   If the Past
has been an obstacle and a burden, knowledge of the Past is the safest and the
surest emancipation.   And the earnest
search for it is one of the signs that dis-
tinguish the four centuries of which I speak
from those that went before.   The middle
ages, which possessed good writers of
contemporary narrative, were careless and
impatient of older fact.   They became

content to be deceived, to live in a twi-
light of fiction, under clouds of false
witness, inventing according to con-
venience, and glad to welcome the forger
and the cheat.[14] As time went on,
the atmosphere of accredited mendacity
thickened, until, in the Renaissance, the
art of exposing falsehood dawned upon
keen Italian minds. It was then that
history as we understand it began to be
understood, and the illustrious dynasty of
scholars arose to whom we still look both
for method and material. Unlike the
dreaming prehistoric world, ours knows the
need and the duty to make itself master of
the earlier times, and to forfeit nothing
of their wisdom or their warnings,[15] and
has devoted its best energy and treasure
to the sovereign purpose of detecting error
and vindicating entrusted truth.[16]

In this epoch of full-grown history men have not acquiesced in the given conditions of their lives. Taking little for granted they have sought to know the ground they stand on, and the road they travel, and the reason why. Over them, therefore, the historian has obtained an increasing ascendancy.[17] The law of stability was overcome by the power of ideas, constantly varied and rapidly renewed ; [18] ideas that give life and motion, that take wing and traverse seas and frontiers, making it futile to pursue the consecutive order of events in the seclusion of a separate nationality.[19] They compel us to share the existence of societies wider than our own, to be familiar with distant and exotic types, to hold our march upon the loftier summits, along the central range, to live in the company of heroes, and saints, and men of genius, that no single country could produce. We cannot afford wantonly to lose sight of great men and memorable lives, and are bound to store up objects for admiration as far as may be ; [20] for the effect of implacable research is constantly to reduce their number. No intellectual exercise, for instance, can be more invigorating than to watch the working of the mind of Napoleon, the most entirely known as well as the ablest of historic men. In another sphere, it is the vision of a higher world to be intimate with the character of Fénelon, the cherished model of politicians, ecclesiastics, and men of letters, the witness against one century and precursor of another, the advocate of the poor against oppression, of liberty in an age of arbitrary power, of tolerance in an age of persecution, of the humane virtues among men accustomed to sacrifice them to authority, the man of whom one enemy says that his cleverness was enough to strike terror, and another, that genius poured in torrents from his eyes. For the minds that are greatest and best alone furnish the instructive examples. A man of ordinary proportion or inferior metal knows not how to think out the rounded circle of his thought, how to divest his will of its surroundings and to rise above the pressure of time and race and circumstance,[21] to choose the star that guides his course, to correct, and test, and assay his convictions by the light within,[22] and, with a resolute conscience and ideal courage, to re-model and reconstitute the character which birth and education gave him.[23]

For ourselves, if it were not the quest of the higher level and the extended horizon, international history would be imposed by the exclusive and insular reason that parliamentary reporting is younger than parliaments. The foreigner has no mystic fabric in his government, and no *arcanum imperii*. For him, the foundations have been laid bare ; every motive and function of the mechanism is accounted for as distinctly as the works of a watch. But with our indigenous constitution, not made with hands or written upon paper, but claiming to develope by a law of organic growth , with our disbelief in the virtue of definitions and general principles and our reliance on relative truths, we can have nothing equivalent to the vivid and prolonged debates in which other communities have displayed the inmost secrets of political science to every man who can read. And the discussions of constituent assemblies, at Philadelphia, Versailles and Paris, at Cadiz and Brussels, at Geneva, Frankfort and Berlin, above nearly all, those of the most enlightened States in the American Union, when they have recast their institutions, are paramount in the literature of politics, and proffer treasures which at home we have never enjoyed.

To historians the later part of their enormous subject is precious because it is inexhaustible. It is the best to know because it is the best known and the most explicit. Earlier scenes stand out from a background of obscurity. We soon reach the sphere of hopeless ignorance and un-profitable doubt. But hundreds and even thousands of the moderns have borne testimony against themselves, and may be studied in their private correspondence and sentenced on their own confession. Their deeds are done in the daylight. Every country opens its archives and invites us to penetrate the mysteries of State. When Hallam wrote his chapter on James II., France was the only Power whose reports were available. Rome followed, and the Hague ; and then came the stores of the Italian States, and at last the Prussian and the Austrian papers, and partly those of Spain. Where Hallam and Lingard were dependent on Barillon, their successors consult the diplomacy of ten governments. The topics indeed are few on which the re-sources have been so employed that we can be content with the work done for us, and never wish it to be done over again.

c

Part of the lives of Luther and Frederic,
a little of the Thirty Years' War, much
of the American Revolution and the
French Restoration, the early years of
Richelieu and Mazarin, and a few
volumes of Mr. Gardiner, show here
and there like Pacific islands in
the ocean. I should not even venture
to claim for Ranke, the real origin-
ator of the heroic study of records,
and the most prompt and fortunate of
European pathfinders, that there is one of
his seventy volumes that has not been
overtaken and in part surpassed. It is
through his accelerating influence mainly
that our branch of study has become progressive, so that the best master is quickly
distanced by the better pupil.[24] The
Vatican archives alone, now made accessible to the world, filled 3,239 cases when

they were sent to France ; and they are not the richest. We are still at the beginning of the documentary age, which will tend to make history independent of historians, to develope learning at the expense of writing, and to accomplish a revolution in other sciences as well.[25]

To men in general I would justify the stress I am laying on modern history, neither by urging its varied wealth, nor the rupture with precedent, nor the perpetuity of change and increase of pace, nor the growing predominance of opinion over belief, and of knowledge over opinion, but by the argument that it is a narrative told of ourselves, the record of a life which is our own, of efforts not yet abandoned to repose, of problems that still entangle the feet and vex the hearts of men. Every part of it is weighty with inestimable lessons that we must learn by experience and at a great price, if we know not how to profit by the example and teaching of those who have gone before us, in a society largely resembling the one we live in.[26]   Its study fulfils its purpose even if it only makes us wiser, without producing books, and gives us the gift of historical thinking, which is better than historical learning.[27]   It is a most powerful ingredient in the formation of character and the training of talent, and our historical judgments have as much to do with hopes of heaven as public or private conduct.   Convictions that have been strained through the instances and the comparisons of modern times differ immeasurably in solidity and force from those which every new fact perturbs, and which are often little better than illusions or unsifted prejudice.[28]

The first of human concerns is religion, and it is the salient feature of the
modern centuries. They are signalised as
the scene of Protestant developments.
Starting from a time of extreme indifference, ignorance, and decline, they were at
once occupied with that conflict which was
to rage so long, and of which no man
could imagine the infinite consequences.
Dogmatic conviction—for I shun to speak
of faith in connection with many characters
of those days—dogmatic conviction rose
to be the centre of universal interest, and
remained down to Cromwell the supreme
influence and motive of public policy. A
time came when the intensity of prolonged
conflict, when even the energy of antago-
nistic assurance, abated somewhat, and the
controversial spirit began to make room
for the scientific ; and as the storm sub-

sided, and the area of settled questions
emerged, much of the dispute was abandoned to the serene and soothing touch
of historians, invested as they are with
the prerogative of redeeming the cause
of religion from many unjust reproaches,
and from the graver evil of reproaches
that are just. Ranke used to say that
Church interests prevailed in politics until
the Seven Years' War, and marked a
phase of society that ended when the
hosts of Brandenburg went into action
at Leuthen, chaunting their Lutheran
hymns.[29] That bold proposition would be
disputed even if applied to the present
age. After Sir Robert Peel had broken up
his party, the leaders who followed him declared that no-popery was the only basis
on which it could be reconstructed.[30] On
the other side may be urged that, in July

1870, at the outbreak of the French war, the only government that insisted on the abolition of the temporal power was Austria ; and since then we have witnessed the fall of Castelar, because he attempted to reconcile Spain with Rome.

Soon after 1850 several of the most intelligent men in France, struck by the arrested increase of their own population and by the telling statistics from Further Britain, foretold the coming preponderance of the English race. They did not foretell, what none could then foresee, the still more sudden growth of Prussia, or that the three most important countries of the globe would, by the end of the century, be those that chiefly belonged to the conquests of the Reformation. So that in Religion, as in so many things, the product of these

centuries has favoured the new elements ;
and the centre of gravity, moving from the
Mediterranean nations to the Oceanic, from
the Latin to the Teuton, has also passed
from the Catholic to the Protestant.[31]

Out of these controversies proceeded
political as well as historical science. It
was in the Puritan phase, before the restoration of the Stuarts, that theology, blend-
ing with politics, effected a fundamental
change. The essentially English reformation of the seventeenth century was less
a struggle between churches than between
sects, often subdivided by questions of
discipline and self-regulation rather than
by dogma. The sectaries cherished no
purpose or prospect of prevailing over the
nations ; and they were concerned with
the individual more than with the con-
gregation, with conventicles, not with

state-churches. Their view was narrowed, but their sight was sharpened. It appeared to them that governments and institutions are made to pass away, like things of earth, whilst souls are immortal ; that there is no more proportion between liberty and power than between eternity and time ; that, therefore, the sphere of enforced command ought to be restricted within fixed limits, and that which had been done by authority, and outward discipline, and organised violence, should be attempted by division of power, and committed to the intellect and the conscience of free men.[32] Thus was exchanged the dominion of will over will for the dominion of reason over reason. The true apostles of toleration are not those who sought protection for their own beliefs, or who had none to protect ; but men to whom, irrespective of their cause, it was a political, a moral, and a theological dogma, a question of conscience, involving both religion and policy.[33] Such a man was Socinus; and others arose in the smaller sects—the Independent founder of the colony of Rhode Island, and the Quaker patriarch of Pennsylvania. Much of the energy and zeal which had laboured for authority of doctrine was employed for liberty of prophesying. The air was filled with the enthusiasm of a new cry; but the cause was still the same. It became a boast that religion was the mother of freedom, that freedom was the lawful offspring of religion; and this transmutation, this subversion of established forms of political life by the development of religious thought, brings us to the heart of my subject, to the significant and central feature of the historic cycle before us. Beginning with the strongest religious movement and the most refined despotism ever known, it has led to the superiority of politics over divinity in the life of nations, and terminates in the equal claim of every man to be unhindered by man in the fulfilment of duty to God [34]—a doctrine laden with storm and havoc, which is the secret essence of the Rights of Man, and the indestructible soul of Revolution.

When we consider what the adverse forces were, their sustained resistance, their frequent recovery, the critical moments when the struggle seemed for ever desperate, in 1685, in 1772, in 1808, it is no hyperbole to say that the progress of the world towards self-government would have been arrested but for the strength afforded by the religious motive in the seven-

teenth century. And this constancy of
progress, of progress in the direction
of organised and assured freedom, is
the characteristic fact of modern history, and its tribute to the theory of
Providence.[35] Many persons, I am well
assured, would detect that this is a
very old story, and a trivial common-
place, and would challenge proof that
the world is making progress in aught
but intellect, that it is gaining in freedom,
or that increase in freedom is either a
progress or a gain. Ranke, who was my
own master, rejected the view that I
have stated ; [36] Comte, the master of better
men, believed that we drag a lengthening
chain under the gathered weight of the
dead hand ; [37] and many of our recent
classics, Carlyle, Newman, Froude, were
persuaded that there is no progress

justifying the ways of God to man, and
that the mere consolidation of liberty is
like the motion of creatures whose advance
is in the direction of their tails. They
deem that anxious precaution against bad
government is an obstruction to good,
and degrades morality and mind by
placing the capable at the mercy of the
incapable, dethroning enlightened virtue
for the benefit of the average man. They
hold that great and salutary things are
done for mankind by power concentrated,
not by power balanced and cancelled
and dispersed, and that the whig theory,
sprung from decomposing sects, the theory
that authority is legitimate only by virtue
of its checks, and that the sovereign
is dependent on the subject, is rebellion
against the divine will manifested all
down the stream of time.

I state the objection not that we may plunge into the crucial controversy of a science that is not identical with ours, but in order to make my drift clear by the defining aid of express contradiction. No political dogma is as serviceable to my purpose here as the historian's maxim to do the best he can for the other side, and to avoid pertinacity or emphasis on his own. Like the economic precept *Laissez-faire* [38] which the eighteenth century derived from Colbert, it has been an important, if not a final step in the making of method. The strongest and most impressive personalities, it is true, like Macaulay, Thiers, and the two greatest of living writers, Mommsen and Treitschke, project their own broad shadow upon their pages. This is a practice proper to great men, and a great man may be worth several immaculate historians. Otherwise there is virtue in the saying that a historian is seen at his best when he does not appear.[39] Better for us is the example of the Bishop of Oxford, who never lets us know what he thinks of anything but the matter before him ; and of his illustrious French rival, Fustel de Coulanges, who said to an excited audience . " Do not imagine you are listening to me ; it is history itself that speaks." [40] We can found no philosophy on the observation of four hundred years, excluding three thousand. It would be an imperfect and a fallacious induction. But I hope that even this narrow and disedifying section of history will aid you to see that the action of Christ who is risen on mankind whom he redeemed fails not, but increases ; [41] that the wisdom of divine rule appears not in

the perfection but in the improvement
of the world ; [42] and that achieved liberty
is the one ethical result that rests on
the converging and combined conditions
of advancing civilisation.[43]   Then you will
understand what a famous philosopher said,
that History is the true demonstration of
Religion.[44]

But what do people mean who proclaim
that liberty is the palm, and the prize,
and the crown, seeing that it is an idea of
which there are two hundred definitions,
and that this wealth of interpretation has
caused more bloodshed than anything,
except theology? Is it Democracy as in
France, or Federalism as in America, or
the national independence which bounds
the Italian view, or the reign of the fittest,
which is the ideal of Germans? [45]   I know
not whether it will ever fall within my

sphere of duty to trace the slow progress
of that idea through the chequered scenes
of our history, and to describe how subtle
speculations touching the nature of conscience promoted a nobler and more
spiritual conception of the liberty that
protects it,[46] until the guardian of rights
developed into the guardian of duties
which are the cause of rights,[47] and that
which had been prized as the material
safeguard for treasures of earth became
sacred as security for things that are divine.
All that we require is a workday key to
history, and our present need can be
supplied without pausing to satisfy philosophers. Without inquiring how far
Sarasa or Butler, Kant or Vinet, is right
as to the infallible voice of God in man,
we may easily agree in this, that where
absolutism reigned, by irresistible arms, con-

centrated possessions, auxiliary churches, and inhuman laws, it reigns no more ; that commerce having risen against land, labour against wealth, the state against the forces dominant in society,[48] the division of power against the state, the thought of individuals against the practice of ages, neither authorities, nor minorities, nor majorities can command implicit obedience ; and, where there has been long and arduous experience, a rampart of tried conviction and accumulated knowledge,[49] where there is a fair level of general morality, education, courage, and self-restraint, there, if there only, a society may be found that exhibits the condition of life towards which, by elimination of failures, the world has been moving through the allotted space.[50] You will know it by outward signs : Representation, the extinction of slavery, the reign of opinion, and the like ; better still by less apparent evidences : the security of the weaker groups [51] and the liberty of conscience, which, effectually secured, secures the rest.

Here we reach a point at which my argument threatens to abut on a contradiction. If the supreme conquests of society are won more often by violence than by lenient arts, if the trend and drift of things is towards convulsions and catastrophes, [52] if the world owes religious liberty to the Dutch Revolution, constitutional government to the English, federal republicanism to the American, political equality to the French and its successors, [53] what is to become of us, docile and attentive students of the absorbing Past ? The triumph of the Revo-

lutionist annuls the historian.[54]   By its
authentic exponents, Jefferson and Sieyès,
the Revolution of the last century repudi-
ates history.   Their followers renounced
acquaintance with it, and were ready to
destroy its records and to abolish its in-
offensive professors.   But the unexpected
truth, stranger than fiction, is that this was
not the ruin but the renovation of history.
Directly and indirectly, by process of development and by process of reaction,
an impulse was given which made it
infinitely more effectual as a factor of
civilisation than ever before, and a movement began in the world of minds which
was deeper and more serious than the
revival of ancient learning.[55]   The dis-
pensation under which we live and labour
consists first in the recoil from the
negative spirit that rejected the law of

growth, and partly in the endeavour to classify and adjust the revolution, and to account for it by the natural working of historic causes. The Conservative line of writers, under the name of the Romantic or Historical School, had its seat in Germany, looked upon the Revolution as an alien episode, the error of an age, a disease to be treated by the investigation of its origin, and strove to unite the broken threads and to restore the normal conditions of organic evolution. The Liberal School, whose home was France, explained and justified the Revolution as a true development, and the ripened fruit of all history.[56] These are the two main arguments of the generation to which we owe the notion and the scientific methods that make history so unlike what it was to the survivors of the

last century.   Severally, the innovators
were not superior to the men of old.
Muratori was as widely read, Tillemont as
accurate, Leibniz as able, Fréret as acute,
Gibbon as masterly in the craft of com-
posite construction.   Nevertheless, in the
second quarter of this century, a new era
began for historians.

I would point to three things in par-
ticular, out of many, which constitute the
amended order.   Of the incessant deluge
of new and unsuspected matter I need
say little.   For some years, the secret
archives of the papacy were accessible
at Paris ; but the time was not ripe,
and almost the only man whom they
availed was the archivist himself. [57]
Towards 1830 the documentary studies
began on a large scale, Austria leading the
way.   Michelet, who claims, towards 1836,

to have been the pioneer,[58] was preceded by such rivals as Mackintosh, Bucholtz, and Mignet. A new and more productive period began thirty years later, when the war of 1859 laid open the spoils of Italy. Every country in succession has now allowed the exploration of its records, and there is more fear of drowning than of drought. The result has been that a lifetime spent in the largest collection of printed books would not suffice to train a real master of modern history. After he had turned from literature to sources, from Burnet to Pocock, from Macaulay to Madame Campana, from Thiers to the interminable correspondence of the Bonapartes, he would still feel instant need of inquiry at Venice or Naples, in the Ossuna library or at the Hermitage.[59]

These matters do not now concern us.

For our purpose, the main thing to learn is not the art of accumulating material, but the sublimer art of investigating it, of discerning truth from falsehood, and certainty from doubt.   It is by solidity of criticism more than by the plenitude of erudition, that the study of history strengthens, and straightens, and extends the mind.[60]   And the accession of the critic in the place of the indefatigable compiler, of the artist in coloured narrative, the skilled limner of character, the persuasive advocate of good, or other, causes, amounts to a transfer of government, to a change of dynasty, in the historic realm. For the critic is one who, when he lights on an interesting statement, begins by suspecting it.   He remains in suspense until he has subjected his authority to three operations.   First, he asks whether

he has read the passage as the author
wrote it. For the transcriber, and the
editor, and the official or officious censor
on the top of the editor, have played
strange tricks, and have much to answer
for. And if they are not to blame, it may
turn out that the author wrote his book
twice over, that you can discover the first
jet, the progressive variations, things
added, and things struck out. Next is the
question where the writer got his information. If from a previous writer, it can be
ascertained, and the inquiry has to be re-
peated. If from unpublished papers, they
must be traced, and when the fountain
head is reached, or the track disappears,
the question of veracity arises. The re-
sponsible writer's character, his position,
antecedents, and probable motives have
to be examined into ; and this is what,

in a different and adapted sense of the word, may be called the higher criticism, in comparison with the servile and often mechanical work of pursuing statements to their root. For a historian has to be treated as a witness, and not believed unless his sincerity is established.[61] The maxim that a man must be presumed to be innocent until his guilt is proved, was not made for him.

For us then the estimate of authorities, the weighing of testimony, is more meritorious than the potential discovery of new matter.[62] And modern history, which is the widest field of application, is not the best to learn our business in ; for it is too wide, and the harvest has not been winnowed as in antiquity, and further on to the Crusades. It is better to examine what has been done for questions that are compact and circumscribed, such as the sources of Plutarch's *Pericles*, the two tracts on Athenian government, the origin of the epistle to Diognetus, the date of the life of St. Antony; and to learn from Schwegler how this analytical work began. More satisfying because more decisive has been the critical treatment of the mediæval writers, parallel with the new editions, on which incredible labour has been lavished, and of which we have no better examples than the prefaces of Bishop Stubbs. An important event in this series was the attack on Dino Compagni, which, for the sake of Dante, roused the best Italian scholars to a not unequal contest. When we are told that England is behind the Continent in critical faculty, we must admit that this is true as to quantity, not as to quality of

work. As they are no longer living, I will
say of two Cambridge professors, Lightfoot
and Hort, that they were critical scholars
whom neither Frenchman nor German has
surpassed.

The third distinctive note of the generation of writers who dug so deep a trench
between history as known to our grand-
fathers and as it appears to us, is their
dogma of impartiality. To an ordinary
man the word means no more than
justice. He considers that he may proclaim the merits of his own religion, of
his prosperous and enlightened country, of
his political persuasion, whether democracy,
or liberal monarchy, or historic conser-
vatism, without transgression or offence,
so long as he is fair to the relative, though
inferior merits of others, and never treats
men as saints or as rogues for the side they

take. There is no impartiality, he would say, like that of a hanging judge. The men who, with the compass of criticism in their hands, sailed the uncharted sea of original research, proposed a different view. History, to be above evasion or dispute, must stand on documents, not on opinions. They had their own notion of truthfulness, based on the exceeding difficulty of finding truth, and the still greater difficulty of impressing it when found. They thought it possible to write, with so much scruple, and simplicity, and insight, as to carry along with them every man of good will, and, whatever his feelings, to compel his assent. Ideas which, in religion and in politics, are truths, in history are forces. They must be respected ; they must not be affirmed. By dint of a supreme reserve, by much self-control, by a timely and discreet indifference, by secrecy in the matter of the black cap, history might be lifted above contention, and made an accepted tribunal, and the same for all.[63] If men were truly sincere, and delivered judgment by no canons but those of evident morality, then Julian would be described in the same terms by Christian and pagan, Luther by Catholic and Protestant, Washington by Whig and Tory, Napoleon by patriotic Frenchman and patriotic German.[64]

I speak of this school with reverence, for the good it has done, by the assertion of historic truth and of its legitimate authority over the minds of men. It provides a discipline which every one of us does well to undergo, and perhaps also well to relinquish. For it is not the whole truth. Lanfrey's essay on Carnot, Chuquet's wars of the

Revolution, Ropes's military histories,
Roget's Geneva in the time of Calvin, will
supply you with examples of a more robust
impartiality than I have described. Renan
calls it the luxury of an opulent and
aristocratic society, doomed to vanish in
an age of fierce and sordid striving. In
our universities it has a magnificent and
appointed refuge ; and to serve its cause,
which is sacred, because it is the cause of
truth and honour, we may import a profit-
able lesson from the highly unscientific
region of public life. There a man does
not take long to find out that he is
opposed by some who are abler and
better than himself. And, in order to
understand the cosmic force and the
true connection of ideas, it is a source
of power, and an excellent school of principle, not to rest until, by excluding the

fallacies, the prejudices, the exaggerations which perpetual contention and the consequent precautions breed, we have made out for our opponents a stronger and more impressive case than they present themselves.[65] Excepting one to which we are coming before I release you, there is no precept less faithfully observed by historians.

Ranke is the representative of the age which instituted the modern study of history. He taught it to be critical, to be colourless, and to be new. We meet him at every step, and he has done more for us than any other man. There are stronger books than any one of his, and some may have surpassed him in political, religious, philosophic insight, in vividness of the creative imagination, in originality, elevation, and depth of thought; but by the extent of important work well executed, by his influence on able men, and by the amount of knowledge which mankind receives and employs with the stamp of his mind upon it, he stands without a rival. I saw him last in 1877, when he was feeble, sunken, and almost blind, and scarcely able to read or write. He uttered his farewell with kindly emotion, and I feared that the next I should hear of him would be the news of his death. Two years later he began a Universal History which is not without traces of weakness, but which, composed after the age of eighty-three, and carried, in seventeen volumes, far into the Middle Ages, brings to a close the most astonishing career in literature.

His course had been determined, in early life, by *Quentin Durward.* The

E

shock of the discovery that Scott's Lewis the Eleventh was inconsistent with the original in Commynes made him resolve that his object thenceforth should be above all things to follow, without swerving, and in stern subordination and surrender, the lead of his authorities. He decided effectually to repress the poet, the patriot, the religious or political partisan, to sustain no cause, to banish himself from his books, and to write nothing that would gratify his own feelings or disclose his private convictions.[66] When a strenuous divine who, like him, had written on the Reformation, hailed him as a comrade, Ranke repelled his advances. " You," he said, " are in the first place a Christian : I am in the first place a historian. There is a gulf between us." [67] He was the first emi- nent writer who exhibited what Michelet calls *le désintéressement des morts*. It was a moral triumph for him when he could refrain from judging, show that much might be said on both sides, and leave the rest to Providence.[68] He would have felt sympathy with the two famous London physicians of our day, of whom it is told that they could not make up their minds on a case and reported dubiously. The head of the family insisted on a positive opinion. They answered that they were unable to give one, but he might easily find fifty doctors who could.

Niebuhr had pointed out that chroniclers who wrote before the invention of printing generally copied one predecessor at a time, and knew little about sifting or combining authorities. The suggestion became luminous in

Ranke's hands, and with his light and dex-
terous touch he scrutinised and dissected
the principal historians, from Machiavelli
to the *Mémoires d'un Homme d'État*, with
a rigour never before applied to moderns.
But whilst Niebuhr dismissed the tradi-
tional story, replacing it with a construction of his own, it was Ranke's mission to
preserve, not to undermine, and to set up
masters whom, in their proper sphere, he
could obey. The many excellent disser-
tations in which he displayed this art,
though his successors in the next generation matched his skill and did still more
thorough work, are the best introduction
from which we can learn the technical
process by which within living memory
the study of modern history has been
renewed. Ranke's contemporaries, weary
of his neutrality and suspense, and of

the useful but subordinate work that was done by beginners who borrowed his wand, thought that too much was made of these obscure preliminaries which a man may accomplish for himself, in the silence of his chamber, with less demand on the attention of the public.[69]   That may be reasonable in men who are practised in these fundamental technicalities.   We who have to learn them, must immerse ourselves in the study of the great examples.

Apart from what is technical, method is only the reduplication of common sense, and is best acquired by observing its use by the ablest men in every variety of intellectual employment.[70]   Bentham acknowledged that he learned less from his own profession than from writers like Linnæus and Cullen; and Brougham advised the student of Law to begin with Dante.

Liebig described his *Organic Chemistry*
as an application of ideas found in Mill's
Logic, and a distinguished physician, not
to be named lest he should overhear me,
read three books to enlarge his medical
mind ; and they were Gibbon, Grote, and
Mill.   He goes on to say, "An educated
man cannot become so on one study alone,
but must be brought under the influence
of natural, civil, and moral modes of
thought." [71]   I quote my colleague's golden
words in order to reciprocate them.   If men
of science owe anything to us, we may learn
much from them that is essential.[72]   For
they can show how to test proof, how to
secure fulness and soundness in induction,
how to restrain and to employ with safety
hypothesis and analogy.   It is they who
hold the secret of the mysterious property
of the mind by which error ministers to

truth, and truth slowly but irrevocably pre-
vails.[73]   Theirs is the logic of discovery,[74]
the demonstration of the advance of knowledge and the development of ideas, which
as the earthly wants and passions of men
remain almost unchanged, are the charter
of progress, and the vital spark in history.
And they often give us invaluable counsel
when they attend to their own subjects
and address their own people.   Remember
Darwin, taking note only of those passages
that raised difficulties in his way ; the
French philosopher complaining that his
work stood still, because he found no more
contradicting facts ; Baer, who thinks error
treated thoroughly, nearly as remunerative
as truth, by the discovery of new objections ; for, as Sir Robert Ball warns us,
it is by considering objections that we
often learn.[75]   Faraday declares that " in

knowledge, that man only is to be con-
demned and despised who is not in a
state of transition." And John Hunter
spoke for all of us, when he said : "Never
ask me what I have said or what I have
written ; but if you will ask me what my
present opinions are, I will tell you."

From the first years of the century we
have been quickened and enriched by
contributors from every quarter. The
jurists brought us that law of continuous
growth which has transformed history
from a chronicle of casual occurrences
into the likeness of something organic.[76]
Towards 1820 divines began to recast
their doctrines on the lines of development, of which Newman said, long after,
that evolution had come to confirm it.[77]
Even the Economists, who were practical
men, dissolved their science into liquid

history, affirming that it is not an auxiliary, but the actual subject-matter of their inquiry.[78]   Philosophers claim that, as early as 1804, they began to bow the metaphysical neck beneath the historical yoke. They taught that philosophy is only the amended sum of all philosophies, that systems pass with the age whose impress they bear,[79] that the problem is to focus the rays of wandering but extant truth, and that history is the source of philosophy, if not quite a substitute for it [80] Comte begins a volume with the words that the preponderance of history over philosophy was the characteristic of the time he lived in.[81]   Since Cuvier first recognised the conjunction between the course of inductive discovery and the course of civilization,[82] science had its share in saturating the age with historic ways of thought, and subjecting all things to that influence for which the depressing names historicism and historical-mindedness have been devised.

There are certain faults which are corrigible mental defects on which I ought to say a few denouncing words, because they are common to us all. First : the want of an energetic understanding of the sequence and real significance of events, which would be fatal to a practical politician, is ruin to a student of history who is the politician with his face turned backwards. [83] It is playing at study, to see nothing but the unmeaning and unsuggestive surface, as we generally do. Then we have a curious proclivity to neglect, and by degrees to forget, what has been certainly known. An instance or two will explain my idea. The

most popular English writer relates how
it happened in his presence that the title
of Tory was conferred upon the Conservative party. For it was an opprobrious
name at the time, applied to men for whom
the Irish Government offered head-money ,
so that if I have made too sure of progress, I may at least complacently point
to this instance of our mended manners.
One day, Titus Oates lost his temper
with the men who refused to believe
him, and after looking about for a scorch-
ing imprecation, he began to call them
Tories.[84] The name remained ; but its
origin, attested by Defoe, dropped out
of common memory, as if one party were
ashamed of their godfather, and the other
did not care to be identified with his cause
and character. You all know, I am sure,
the story of the news of Trafalgar, and

how, two days after it had arrived, Mr.
Pitt, drawn by an enthusiastic crowd, went
to dine in the city. When they drank the
health of the minister who had saved his
country, ne declined the praise. " England," he said, "has saved herself by her
own energy; and I hope that after having
saved herself by her energy, she will save
Europe by her example." In 1814, when
this hope had been realised, the last speech
of the great orator was remembered, and
a medal was struck upon which the
whole sentence was engraved, in four
words of compressed Latin : " *Seipsam
virtute, Europam exemplo.*" Now it
was just at the time of his last appear-
ance in public that Mr. Pitt heard of the
overwhelming success of the French in
Germany, and of the Austrian surrender
at Ulm. His friends concluded that the

contest on land was hopeless, and that it was time to abandon the Continent to the conqueror, and to fall back upon our new empire of the sea. Pitt did not agree with them. He said that Napoleon would meet with a check whenever he encountered a national resistance; and he declared that Spain was the place for it, and that then England would intervene.[85] General Wellesley, fresh from India, was present. Ten years later, when he had accomplished that which Pitt had seen in the lucid prescience of his last days, he related at Paris what I scarcely hesitate to call the most astounding and profound prediction in all political history, where such things have not been rare.

I shall never again enjoy the opportunity of speaking my thoughts to such an audience as this, and on so privileged an occasion a lecturer may well be tempted to bethink himself whether he knows of any neglected truth, any cardinal proposition, that might serve as his selected epigraph, as a last signal, perhaps even as a target. I am not thinking of those shining precepts which are the registered property of every school ; that is to say—Learn as much by writing as by reading; be not content with the best book ; seek sidelights from the others ; have no favourites ; keep men and things apart; guard against the prestige of great names ;[86] see that your judgments are your own, and do not shrink from disagreement ; no trusting without testing ; be more severe to ideas than to actions ;[87] do not overlook the strength of the bad cause or the weakness of the good ;[88] never be

surprised by the crumbling of an idol or
the disclosure of a skeleton ; judge talent
at its best and character at its worst ;
suspect power more than vice,[89] and study
problems in preference to periods ; for
instance : the derivation of Luther, the
scientific influence of Bacon, the prede-
cessors of Adam Smith, the mediæval
masters of Rousseau, the consistency of
Burke, the identity of the first Whig.
Most of this, I suppose, is undisputed, and
calls for no enlargement. But the weight
of opinion is against me when I exhort
you never to debase the moral currency or
to lower the standard of rectitude, but to
try others by the final maxim that governs
your own lives, and to suffer no man and no
cause to escape the undying penalty which
history has the power to inflict on wrong.[90]
The plea in extenuation of guilt and mitiga-

tion of punishment is perpetual. At every step we are met by arguments which go to excuse, to palliate, to confound right and wrong, and reduce the just man to the level of the reprobate. The men who plot to baffle and resist us are, first of all, those who made history what it has become. They set up the principle that only a foolish Conservative judges the present time with the ideas of the Past; that only a foolish Liberal judges the Past with the ideas of the Present.[91]

The mission of that school was to make distant times, and especially the middle ages, then most distant of all, intelligible and acceptable to a society issuing from the eighteenth century. There were difficulties in the way; and among others this, that, in the first fervour of the Crusades, the men who took the Cross, after receiving communion, heartily devoted the day to the extermination of Jews. To judge them by a fixed standard, to call them sacrilegious fanatics or furious hypocrites, was to yield a gratuitous victory to Voltaire. It became a rule of policy to praise the spirit when you could not defend the deed. So that we have no common code ; our moral notions are always fluid ; and you must consider the times, the class from which men sprang, the surrounding influences, the masters in their schools, the preachers in their pulpits, the movement they obscurely obeyed, and so on, until responsibility is merged in numbers, and not a culprit is left for execution.[92] A murderer was no criminal if he followed local custom, if neighbours approved, if he was encouraged by official

F

advisers or prompted by just authority, if he acted for the reason of state or the pure love of religion, or if he sheltered himself behind the complicity of the Law. The depression of morality was flagrant; but the motives were those which have enabled us to contemplate with distressing complacency the secret of unhallowed lives. The code that is greatly modified by time and place, will vary according to the cause. The amnesty is an artifice that enables us to make exceptions, to tamper with weights and measures, to deal unequal justice to friends and enemies.

It is associated with that philosophy which Cato attributes to the gods. For we have a theory which justifies Providence by the event, and holds nothing so deserving as success, to which there can be no victory in a bad cause, prescription and duration legitimate,[93] and whatever exists is right and reasonable ; and as God manifests His will by that which He tolerates, we must conform to the divine decree by living to shape the Future after the ratified image of the Past.[94] Another theory, less confidently urged, regards History as our guide, as much by showing errors to evade as examples to pursue. It is suspicious of illusions in success, and, though there may be hope of ultimate triumph for what is true, if not by its own attraction, by the gradual exhaustion of error, it admits no corresponding promise for what is ethically right. It deems the canonisation of the historic Past more perilous than ignorance or denial, because it would perpetuate the reign of sin and acknowledge the sovereignty of wrong, and conceives it the

part of real greatness to know how to
stand and fall alone, stemming, for a lifetime, the contemporary flood.[95]

Ranke relates, without adornment, that
William III. ordered the extirpation of a
Catholic clan, and scouts the faltering
excuse of his defenders. But when he
comes to the death and character of the
international deliverer, Glencoe is for-
gotten, the imputation of murder drops, like
a thing unworthy of notice.[96] Johannes
Mueller, a great Swiss celebrity, writes
that the British Constitution occurred to
somebody, perhaps to Halifax. This art-
less statement might not be approved
by rigid lawyers as a faithful and
felicitous indication of the manner of
that mysterious growth of ages, from
occult beginnings, that was never pro-
faned by the invading wit of man ;[97] but

it is less grotesque than it appears. Lord
Halifax was the most original writer of
political tracts in the pamphleteering crowd
between Harrington and Bolingbroke ; and
in the Exclusion struggle he produced
a scheme of limitations which, in substance,
if not in form, foreshadowed the position
of the monarchy in the later Hanoverian
reigns. Although Halifax did not believe
in the Plot,[98] he insisted that innocent
victims should be sacrificed to content the
multitude. Sir William Temple writes :—
" We only disagreed in one point, which
was the leaving some priests to the law
upon the accusation of being priests only,
as the House of Commons had desired ;
which I thought wholly unjust. Upon this
point Lord Halifax and I had so sharp
a debate at Lord Sunderland's lodgings,
that he told me, if I would not concur in

points which were so necessary for the people's satisfaction, he would tell everybody I was a Papist. And upon his affirming that the plot must be handled as if it were true, whether it were so or no, in those points that were so generally believed." In spite of this accusing passage Macaulay, who prefers Halifax to all the statesmen of his age, praises him for his mercy : " His dislike of extremes, and a forgiving and compassionate temper which seems to have been natural to him, preserved him from all participation in the worst crimes of his time."

If, in our uncertainty, we must often err, it may be sometimes better to risk excess in rigour than in indulgence, for then at least we do no injury by loss of principle. As Bayle has said, it is more probable that the secret motives of an indifferent action are

bad than good; [99] and this discouraging
conclusion does not depend upon theology,
for James Mozley supports the sceptic
from the other flank, with all the artillery
of Tractarian Oxford "A Christian," he
says, "is bound by his very creed to suspect evil, and cannot release himself. . . .
He sees it where others do not; his instinct
is divinely strengthened, his eye is super-
naturally keen; he has a spiritual insight,
and senses exercised to discern . . He
owns the doctrine of original sin, that doctrine puts him necessarily on his guard
against appearances, sustains his apprehension under perplexity, and prepares
him for recognising anywhere what he
knows to be everywhere." [100] There is
a popular saying of Madame de Stael,
that we forgive whatever we really
understand. The paradox has been

judiciously pruned by her descendant, the Duke de Broglie, in the words: " Beware of too much explaining, lest we end by too much excusing." [101] History, says Froude, does teach that right and wrong are real distinctions. Opinions alter, manners change, creeds rise and fall, but the moral law is written on the tablets of eternity.[102] And if there are moments when we may resist the teaching of Froude, we have seldom the chance of resisting when he is supported by Mr. Goldwin Smith : " A sound historical morality will sanction strong measures in evil times ; selfish ambition, treachery, murder, perjury, it will never sanction in the worst of times, for these are the things that make times evil.—Justice has been justice, mercy has been mercy, honour has been honour, good faith has been

good faith, truthfulness has been truthfulness from the beginning." The
doctrine that, as Sir Thomas Browne
says, morality is not ambulatory,[103] is ex-
pressed as follows by Burke, who, when
true to himself, is the most intelligent of our
instructors : " My principles enable me to
form my judgment upon men and actions
in history, just as they do in common life ,
and are not formed out of events and
characters, either present or past. History
is a preceptor of prudence, not of principles.
The principles of true politics are those
of morality enlarged ; and I neither now
do, nor ever will admit of any other." [104]

Whatever a man's notions of these later
centuries are, such, in the main, the man
himself will be. Under the name of History, they cover the articles of his philosophic, his religious, and his political

creed.[105]   They give his measure ; they
denote his character : and, as praise is the
shipwreck of historians, his preferences
betray   him   more   than   his   aversions.
Modern history touches us so nearly, it
is so deep a question of life and death,
that we are bound to find our own way
through it, and to owe our insight to
ourselves.   The historians of former ages,
unapproachable for us in knowledge and
in talent, cannot be our limit.   We have
the power to be more rigidly impersonal,
disinterested and just than they ; and to
learn from undisguised and genuine records to look with remorse upon the past,
and to the future with assured hope of
better things ; bearing this in mind, that
if we lower our standard in history, we
cannot uphold it in Church or State

NOTES

[1] No political conclusions of any value for practice can be arrived at by direct experience. All true political science is, in one sense of the phrase, *a priori*, being deduced from the tendencies of things, tendencies known either through our general experience of human nature, or as the result of an analysis of the course of history, considered as a progressive evolution. —MILL, *Inaugural Address*, 51.

[2] Contemporary history is, in Dr Arnold's opinion, more important than either ancient or modern , and in fact superior to it by all the superiority of the end to the means —SEELEY, *Lectures and Essays*, 306.

[3] The law of all progress is one and the same, the evolution of the simple into the complex by successive differentiations.—*Edinburgh Review*, clvii 428. Die Entwickelung der Volker vollzieht sich nach zwei Gesetzen   Das erste Gesetz ist das der Differenzierung. Die primitiven Einrichtungen sind einfach und einheitlich, die der Civilisation zusammengesetzt und geteilt, und die Arbeitsteilung nimmt bestandig zu.—SICKEL, *Goettingen Gelehrte Anzeigen*, 1890, 563.

[4] Nous risquons toujours d'être influencés par les

préjugés de notre époque , mais nous sommes libres
des préjugés particuliers aux époques antérieures —
E Naville, *Christianisme de Fénelon*, 9

⁵ La nature n'est qu'un écho de l'esprit. L'idée
est la mère du fait, elle façonne graduellement le
monde à son image —Feuchtersleben, *in* Caro,
Nouvelles Études Morales, 132. Il n'est pas d'étude
morale qui vaille l'histoire d'une idée.—Laboulaye,
Liberté Religieuse, 25.

⁶ Il y a des savants qui raillent le sentiment religieux. Ils ne savent pas que c'est à ce sentiment, et
par son moyen, que la science historique doit d'avoir
pu sortir de l'enfance. . . . Depuis des siècles les âmes
indépendantes discutaient les textes et les traditions
de l'église, quand les lettrés n'avaient pas encore eu
l'idée de porter un regard critique sur les textes de
l'antiquité mondaine.—*La France Protestante*, 11 17.

⁷ In our own history, above all, every step in advance has been at the same time a step backwards
It has often been shown how our latest constitution
is, amidst all external differences, essentially the same
as our earliest, how every struggle for right and freedom, from the thirteenth century onwards, has simply
been a struggle for recovering something old —
Freeman, *Historical Essays*, IV. 253. Nothing but a
thorough knowledge of the social system, based
upon a regular study of its growth, can give us the
power we require to affect it.—Harrison, *Meaning of
History*, 19. Eine Sache wird nur völlig auf dem
Wege verstanden, wie sie selbst entsteht.—In dem
genetischen Verfahren sind die Grunde der Sache,

auch die Grunde des Erkennens —TRENDELENBURG,
Logische Untersuchungen, ii. 395, 388

[8] Une telle liberté . . . n'a rien de commun avec
le savant système de garanties qui fait libres les peuples
modernes.—BOUTMY, *Annales des Sciences Politiques*,
i. 157. Les trois grandes réformes qui ont renouvelé
l'Angleterre, la liberté religieuse, la réforme parle-
mentaire, et la liberté économique, ont été obtenues
sous la pression des organisations extra-constitution-
nelles.—OSTROGORSKI, *Revue Historique*, lii. 272.

[9] The question which is at the bottom of all
constitutional struggles, the question between the
national will and the national law.—GARDINER,
Documents, xviii. Religion, considered simply as the
principle which balances the power of human opinion,
which takes man out of the grasp of custom and
fashion, and teaches him to refer himself to a higher
tribunal, is an infinite aid to moral strength and
elevation.—CHANNING, *Works*, iv. 83. Je tiens que
le passé ne suffit jamais au présent. Personne n'est
plus disposé que moi à profiter de ses leçons, mais
en même temps, je le demande, le présent ne fournit-il
pas toujours les indications qui lui sont propres?—
MOLÉ, *in* FALLOUX, *Études et Souvenirs*, 130 Admirons
la sagesse de nos pères, et tachons de l'imiter, en
faisant ce qui convient à notre siècle.—GALIANI,
Dialogues, 40.

[10] Ceterum in legendis Historiis malim te ductum
animi, quam anxias leges sequi Nullae sunt, quae
non magnas habeant utilitates; et melius haerent,
quae libenter legimus In universum tamen, non
incipere ab antiquissimis, sed ab his, quae nostris

temporibus nostraeque notitiae propius cohaerent, ac paulatim deinde in remotiora eniti, magis è re arbitror. —GROTIUS, *Epistolæ*, 18.

[11] The older idea of a law of degeneracy, of a " fatal drift towards the worse," is as obsolete as astrology or the belief in witchcraft. The human race has become hopeful, sanguine —SEELEY, *Rede Lecture*, 1887. *Fortnightly Review*, July, 1887, 124

[12] Formuler des idées générales, c'est changer le salpêtre en poudre.—A. DE MUSSET, *Confessions d'un Enfant du Siècle*, 15 Les révolutions c'est l'avènement des idées libérales C'est presque toujours par les révolutions qu'elles prévalent et se fondent, et quand les idées libérales en sont véritablement le principe et le but, quand elles leur ont donné naissance, et quand elles les couronnent à leur dernier jour, alors ces révolutions sont légitimes—RÉMUSAT, 1839, in *Revue des Deux Mondes*, 1875, vi. 335. Il y a même des personnes de piété qui prouvent par raison qu'il faut renoncer à la raison, que ce n'est point la lumière, mais la foi seule qui doit nous conduire, et que l'obéissance aveugle est la principale vertu des chrétiens. · La paresse des inférieurs et leur esprit flatteur s'accommode souvent de cette vertu prétendue, et l'orgueil de ceux qui commandent en est toujours très content De sorte qu'il se trouvera peut-être des gens qui seront scandalisés que je fasse cet honneur à la raison, de l'élever au-dessus de toutes les puissances, et qui s'imagineront que je me révolte contre les autorités légitimes à cause que je prends son parti et que je soutiens que c'est à elle à décider et à regner.— MALEBRANCHE, *Morale*, 1 2, 13. That great statesman

(Mr. Pitt) distinctly avowed that the application of philosophy to politics was at that time an innovation, and that it was an innovation worthy to be adopted. He was ready to make the same avowal in the present day which Mr. Pitt had made in 1792 —CANNING, June 1, 1827. *Parliamentary Review*, 1828, 71. American history knows but one avenue of success in American legislation, freedom from ancient prejudice The best lawgivers in our colonies first became as little children.—BANCROFT, *History of the United States*, 1. 494.—Every American, from Jefferson and Gallatin down to the poorest squatter, seemed to nourish an idea that he was doing what he could to overthrow the tyranny which the past had fastened on the human mind —ADAMS, *History of the United States*, 1. 175.

[13] The greatest changes of which we have had experience as yet are due to our increasing knowledge of history and nature. They have been produced by a few minds appearing in three or four favoured nations, in comparatively a short period of time. May we be allowed to imagine the minds of men everywhere working together during many ages for the completion of our knowledge? May not the increase of knowledge transfigure the world? — JOWETT, *Plato*, 1. 414 Nothing, I believe, is so likely to beget in us a spirit of enlightened liberality, of Christian forbearance, of large-hearted moderation, as the careful study of the history of doctrine and the history of interpretation.—PEROWNE, *Psalms*, 1. p xxxi.

[14] Ce n'est guère avant la seconde moitié du XVIIᵉ

siècle qu'il devint impossible de soutenir l'authenticité des fausses décrétales, des Constitutions apostoliques, des Récognitions Clémentines, du faux Ignace, du pseudo-Dionys, et de l'immense fatras d'œuvres anonymes ou pseudonymes qui grossissait souvent du tiers ou de la moitié l'héritage littéraire des auteurs les plus considérables.—DUCHESNE, *Témoins anténicéens de la Trinité*, 1883, 36

[15] A man who does not know what has been thought by those who have gone before him is sure to set an undue value upon his own ideas.—M. PATTISON, *Memoirs*, 78

[16] Travailler à discerner, dans cette discipline, le solide d'avec le frivole, le vrai d'avec le vraisemblable, la science d'avec l'opinion, ce qui forme le jugement d'avec ce qui ne fait que charger la mémoire.—LAMY, *Connoissance de soi-même*, v. 459.

[17] All our hopes of the future depend on a sound understanding of the past.—HARRISON, *The Meaning of History*, 6

[18] The real history of mankind is that of the slow advance of resolved deed following laboriously just thought, and all the greatest men live in their purpose and effort more than it is possible for them to live in reality.—The things that actually happened were of small consequence—the thoughts that were developed are of infinite consequence —RUSKIN. Facts are the mere dross of history. It is from the abstract truth which interpenetrates them, and lies latent among them like gold in the ore, that the mass derives its value —MACAULAY, *Works*, v. 131.

[19] Die Gesetze der Geschichte sind eben die Gesetze der ganzen Menschheit, gehen nicht in die Geschicke eines Volkes, einer Generation oder gar eines Einzelnen auf Individuen und Geschlechter, Staaten und Nationen, konnen zerstauben, die Menschheit bleibt —A. SCHMIDT, *Zuricher Monatschrift*. 1. 45.

[20] Le grand péril des âges démocratiques, soyez-en sûr, c'est la destruction ou l'affaiblissement excessif des parties du corps social en présence du tout. Tout ce qui relève de nos jours l'idée de l'individu est sain.—TOCQUEVILLE, Jan 3, 1840, *Œuvres*, vii. 97. En France, il n'y a plus d'hommes On a systématiquement tué l'homme au profit du peuple, des masses, comme disent nos législateurs écervelés. Puis un beau jour, on s'est aperçu que ce peuple n'avait jamais existé qu'en projet, que ces masses étaient un troupeau mi-partie de moutons et de tigres C'est une triste histoire. Nous avons à relever l'âme humaine contre l'aveugle et brutale tyrannie des multitudes. —LANFREY, March 23, 1855. M DU CAMP, *Souvenirs Littéraires*, ii. 273. C'est le propre de la vertu d'être invisible, même dans l'histoire, à tout autre œil que celui de la conscience.—VACHEROT, *Comptes Rendus de l'Institut*, lxix. 319. Dans l'histoire où la bonté est la perle rare, qui a été bon passe presque avant qui a été grand.—V. HUGO, *Les Misérables*, vii. 46. Grosser Maenner Leben und Tod der Wahrheit gemaess mit Liebe zu schildern, ist zu allen Zeiten herzerhebend , am meisten aber dann, wenn im Kreislauf der irdischen Dinge die Sterne wieder

aehnlich stehen wie damals als sie unter uns lebten.—
LASAULX, *Sokrates*, 3. Instead of saying that the
history of mankind is the history of the masses, it
would be much more true to say that the history of
mankind is the history of its great men.—KINGSLEY,
Lectures, 329

[21] Le génie n'est que la plus complète émancipation
de toutes les influences de temps, de mœurs et de
pays —NISARD, *Souvenirs*, ii. 43.

[22] Meine kritische Richtung zieht mich in der
Wissenschaft durchaus zur Kritik meiner eigenen
Gedanken hin, nicht zu der der Gedanken Anderer.—
ROTHE, *Ethik*, i , p. xi.

[23] When you are in young years the whole mind is,
as it were, fluid, and is capable of forming itself into
any shape that the owner of the mind pleases to order it
to form itself into.—CARLYLE, *On the Choice of Books*,
131   Nach allem erscheint es somit unzweifelhaft
als eine der psychologischen Voraussetzungen des
Strafrechts, ohne welche der Zurechnungsbegriff nicht
haltbar ware, dass der Mensch für seinen Charakter
verantwortlich ist und ihn muss abandern konnen.
—RUMELIN, *Reden und Aufsatze*, ii., 60. An der tiefen
und verborgenen Quelle, woraus der Wille entspringt,
an diesem Punkt, nur hier steht die Freiheit, und
fuhrt das Steuer und lenkt den Willen. Wer nicht
bis zu dieser Tiefe in sich einkehren und seinen
naturlichen Charakter von hier aus bemeistern kann,
der hat nicht den Gebrauch seiner Freiheit, der ist
nicht frei, sondern unterworfen dem Triebwerk seiner
Interessen, und dadurch in der Gewalt des Weltlaufs,

worin jede Begebenheit und jede Handlung eine nothwendige Folge ist aller vorhergehenden.— FISCHER, *Problem der Freiheit*, 27.

[24] I must regard the main duty of a Professor to consist, not simply in communicating information, but in doing this in such a manner, and with such an accompaniment of subsidiary means, that the information he conveys may be the occasion of awakening his pupils to a vigorous and varied exertion of their faculties —SIR W. HAMILTON, *Lectures*, i. 14 No great man really does his work by imposing his maxims on his disciples, he evokes their life. The pupil may become much wiser than his instructor, he may not accept his conclusions, but he will own, "You awakened me to be myself, for that I thank you"— MAURICE, *The Conscience*, 7, 8.

[25] Ich sehe die Zeit kommen, wo wir die neuere Geschichte nicht mehr auf die Berichte selbst nicht der gleichzeitigen Historiker, ausser in so weit ihnen neue originale Kenntniss beiwohnte, geschweige denn auf die weiter abgeleiteten Bearbeitungen zu grunden haben, sondern aus den Relationen der Augenzeugen und der achten und unmittelbarsten Urkunden aufbauen werden.—RANKE, *Reformation*, *Preface*, 1838. Ce qu'on a trouvé et mis en œuvre est considérable en soi c'est peu de chose au prix de ce qui reste à trouver et à mettre en œuvre.—AULARD, *Études sur la Révolution*, 21.

[26] N'attendez donc pas les leçons de l'expérience ; elles coûtent trop cher aux nations.—O. BARROT, *Mémoires* ii 435. Il y a des leçons dans tous les temps,

pour tous les temps, et celles qu'on emprunte à des ennemis ne sont pas les moins précieuses.—LANFREY, *Napoléon*, v. p 11. Old facts may always be fresh, and may give out a fresh meaning for each generation, —MAURICE, *Lectures*, 62. The object is to lead the student to attend to them, to make him take interest in history not as a mere narrative, but as a chain of causes and effects still unwinding itself before our eyes, and full of momentous consequences to himself and his descendants—an unremitting conflict between good and evil powers, of which every act done by any one of us, insignificant as we are, forms one of the incidents, a conflict in which even the smallest of us cannot escape from taking part, in which whoever does not help the right side is helping the wrong —MILL, *Inaugural Address*, 59

[27] I hold that the degree in which Poets dwell in sympathy with the Past, marks exactly the degree of their poetical faculty.—WORDSWORTH in C. FOX, *Memoirs*, June, 1842. In all political, all social, all human questions whatever, history is the main resource of the inquirer.—HARRISON, *Meaning of History*, 15. There are no truths which more readily gain the assent of mankind, or are more firmly retained by them, than those of an historical nature, depending upon the testimony of others —PRIESTLEY, *Letters to French Philosophers*, 9. Improvement consists in bringing our opinions into nearer agreement with facts, and we shall not be likely to do this while we look at facts only through glasses coloured by those very opinions. —MILL, *Inaugural Address*, 25

[28] He who has learnt to understand the true charac
ter and tendency of many succeeding ages is not likely
to go very far wrong in estimating his own.—LECKY,
Value of History, 21. C'est à l'histoire qu'il faut se
prendre, c'est le fait que nous devons interroger, quand
l'idée vacille et fuit à nos yeux —MICHELET, *Disc.
d'Ouverture*, 263 C'est la loi des faits telle qu'elle
se manifeste dans leur succession. C'est la règle de
conduite donnée par la nature humaine et indiquée par
l'histoire C'est la logique, mais cette logique qui ne
fait qu'un avec l'enchaînement des choses. C'est
l'enseignement de l'expérience.—SCHERER, *Mélanges*
558. Wer seine Vergangenheit nicht als seine
Geschichte hat und weiss wird und ist characterlos
Wem ein Ereigniss sein Sonst plötzlich abreisst von
seinem Jetzt wird leicht wurzellos —KLIEFOTH,
Rheinwalds Repertorium, xliv. 20. La politique
est une des meilleures écoles pour l'esprit. Elle force
à chercher la raison de toutes choses, et ne permet pas
cependant de la chercher hors des faits.—RÉMUSAT,
Le Temps Passé, i. 31. It is an unsafe partition that
divides opinions without principle from unprincipled
opinions.—COLERIDGE, *Lay Sermon*, 373.

> Wer nicht von drei tausend Jahren sich weiss Rechenschaft
>   zu geben,
> Bleib' im Dunkeln unerfahren, mag von Tag zu Tage leben !
>   GOETHE

What can be rationally required of the student of
philosophy is not a preliminary and absolute, but a
gradual and progressive, abrogation of prejudices.—
SIR W. HAMILTON, *Lectures*, iv. 92

²⁹ Die Schlacht bei Leuthen ist wohl die letzte, in welcher diese religiosen Gegensatze entscheidend einge-wirkt haben.—RANKE, *Allgemeine Deutsche Biographie*, vii. 70.

³⁰ The only real cry in the country is the proper and just old No Popery cry.—*Major Beresford*, July, 1847. Unfortunately the strongest bond of union amongst them is an apprehension of Popery —*Stanley*, September 12, 1847. The great Protectionist party having degenerated into a No Popery, No Jew Party, I am still more unfit now than I was in 1846 to lead it.—*G. Bentinck*, December 26, 1847 *Croker's Memoirs*, iii 116, 132, 157

³¹ In the case of Protestantism, this constitutional instability is now a simple matter of fact, which has become too plain to be denied. The system is not fixed, but in motion, and the motion is for the time in the direction of complete self-dissolution —We take it for a transitory scheme, whose breaking up is to make room in due time for another and far more perfect state of the Church —The new order in which Pro-testantism is to become thus complete cannot be reached without the co-operation and help of Romanism —NEVIN, *Mercersburg Review*, iv. 48.

³² Diese Heiligen waren es, die aus dem unmittel-baren Glaubensleben und den Grundgedanken der christlichen Freiheit zuerst die Idee allgemeiner Menschenrechte abgeleitet und rein von Selbstsucht vertheidigt haben —WEINGARTEN, *Revolutionskirchen*, 447. Wie selbst die Idee allgemeiner Menschenrechte, die in dem gemeinsamen Character der Ebenbildlich-

keıt Gottes gegrundet sınd, erst durch das Chrısten-
thum zum Bewusstseın gebracht werden, wahrend ʝeder
andere Eıfer fur polıtısche Freıheıt als eın mehr oder
wenıger selbstsuchtıger und beschrankter sich erwiesen
hat.—NEANDER, *Pref. to Uhden's Wılberforce*, p v
The rıghts of ındıvıduals and the ʝustıce due to them
are as dear and precıous as those of states, indeed
the latter are founded on the former, and the great
end and obʝect of them must be to secure and support
the rıghts of ındıvıduals, or else vaın is government.
—CUSHING ın CONWAY, *Lıfe of Paıne*, ı. 217. As ıt
is owned the whole scheme of Scrıpture ıs not yet
understood ; so, ıf ıt ever comes to be understood,
before the restıtutıon of all thıngs, and wıthout mıracu-
lous ınterposıtıons, ıt ınust be ın the same way as
natuıal knowledge ıs come at—by the contınuance
and progress of learnıng and lıberty.—BUTLER,
Analogy, ıı. 3.

³³ Comme les loıs elles-mêmes sont faıllıbles, et qu'ıl
peut y avoır une autre ʝustıce que la ʝustıce écrıte,
les socıétés modernes ont voulu garantır les droıts de
la conscıence à la poursuıte d'une justıce meılleure que
celle quı exıste, et là est le fondement de ce qu'on
appelle lıberté de conscıence, lıberté d'écrıre, lıberté
de pensée —JANET, *Phılosophıe Contemporaine*, 308.
Sı la force matérıelle a touʝours finı par céder à
l'opınıon, combıen plus ne sera-t-elle pas contraınte de
céder à la conscıence ? Car la conscıence, c'est l'opınıon
renforcée par le sentıment de l'oblıgatıon —VINET,
Lıberté Relıgıeuse, 3

³⁴ Après la volonté d'un homme, la raıson d'état,

après la raison d'état, la religion , après la religion, la
liberté. Voilà toute la philosophie de l'histoire —
FLOTTES, *La Souveraineté du Peuple*, 1851, 192. La
répartition plus égale des biens et des droits dans ce
monde est le plus grand objet que doivent se proposer
ceux qui mènent les affaires humaines. Je veux seulement que l'égalité en politique consiste à être également
libre —TOCQUEVILLE, September 10, 1856. *Mme*
Swetchine, 1. 455 On peut concevoir une législation très simple, lorsqu'on voudra en écarter tout ce
qui est arbitraire, ne consulter que les deux premières
lois de la liberté et de la propriété, et ne point ad-
mettre de lois positives qui ne tirent leur raison de
ces deux lois souveraines de la justice essentielle et
absolue —LETROSNE, *Vues sur la Justice Criminelle*, 16.
Summa enim libertas est, ad optimum recta ratione
cogi —Nemo optat sibi hanc libertatem, volendi quae
velit, sed potius volendi optima —LEIBNIZ, *De Fato*
TRENDELENBURG, *Beitrage zur Philosophie*, 11. 190.

[35] All the world is, by the very law of its creation,
in eternal progress , and the cause of all the evils of
the world may be traced to that natural, but most
deadly error of human indolence and corruption, that
our business is to preserve and not to improve —
ARNOLD, *Life*, 1 259. In whatever state of knowledge we may conceive man to be placed, his progress
towards a yet higher state need never fear a check,
but must continue till the last existence of society.—
HERSCHEL, *Prel Dis* , 360. It is in the development of thought as in every other development , the
present suffers from the past, and the future struggles

hard in escaping from the present.—MAX MULLER, *Science of Thought*, 617. Most of the great positive evils of the world are in themselves removable, and will, if human affairs continue to improve, be in the end reduced within narrow limits. Poverty in any sense implying suffering may be completely extinguished by the wisdom of society combined with the good sense and providence of individuals —All the grand sources, in short, of human suffering are in a great degree, many of them almost entirely, conquerable by human care and effort.—J. S MILL, *Utilitarianism*, 21, 22 The ultimate standard of worth is personal worth, and the only progress that is worth striving after, the only acquisition that is truly good and enduring, is the growth of the soul —BIXBY, *Crisis of Morals*, 210. La science, et l'industrie qu'elle produit, ont, parmi tous les autres enfants du génie de l'homme, ce privilége particulier, que leur vol non-seulement ne peut pas s'interrompre, mais qu'il s'accélère sans cesse.—CUVIER, *Discours sur la Marche des Sciences*, 24 Avril, 1816. Aucune idée parmi celles qui se réfèrent à l'ordre des faits naturels, ne tient de plus près à la famille des idées religieuses que l'idée du progrès, et n'est plus propre à devenir le principe d'une sorte de foi religieuse pour ceux qui n'en ont pas d'autres. Elle a, comme la foi religieuse, la vertu de relever les âmes et les caractères —COURNOT, *Marche des Idées*, ii. 425. Dans le spectacle de l'humanité errante, souffrante et travaillant toujours à mieux voir, à mieux penser, à mieux agir, à diminuer l'infirmité de l'être humain, à apaiser l'inquiétude de son cœur, la science découvre une direction et un progrès.—A. SOREL, *Discours de Réception*, 14. Le jeune homme qui commence son éducation quinze ans après son père, à une époque où celui-ci, engagé dans une profession spéciale et active, ne peut que suivre les anciens principes, acquiert une supériorité théorique dont on doit tenir compte dans la hiérarchie sociale. Le plus souvent le père n'est-il pas pénétré de l'esprit de routine, tandis que le fils représente et défend la science progressive ? En diminuant l'écart qui existait entre l'influence des jeunes générations et celle de la vieillesse ou de l'âge mûr, les peuples modernes n'auraient donc fait que reproduire dans leur ordre social un changement de rapports qui s'était déjà accompli dans la nature intime des choses.— BOUTMY, *Revue Nationale*, XXI. 393. Il y a dans l'homme individuel des principes de progrès viager, il y a, en toute société, des causes constantes qui transforment ce progrès viager en progrès héréditaire. Une société quelconque tend à progresser tant que les circonstances ne touchent pas aux causes de progrès que nous avons reconnues, l'imitation des dévanciers par les successeurs, des étrangers par les indigènes.—LACOMBE, *L'Histoire comme Science*, 292. Veram creatæ mentis beatitudinem consistere in non impedito progressu ad bona majora —LEIBNIZ to WOLF, February 21, 1705. In cumulum etiam pulchritudinis perfectionisque universalis operum divinorum progressus quidam perpetuus liberrimusque totius universi est agnoscendus, ita ut ad majorem semper cultum

procedat.—LEIBNIZ ed. Erdmann, 150a Der Creaturen
und also auch unsere Vollkommenheit bestehet in
einem ungehinderten starken Forttrieb zu neuen und
neuen Vollkommenheiten.—LEIBNIZ, *Deutsche Schrift-
en,* II 36. Hegel, welcher annahm, der Fortschritt
der Neuzeit gegen das Mittelalter sei dieser, dass die
Principien der Tugend und des Christenthums,
welche im Mittelalter sich allein im Privatleben und
der Kirche zur Geltung gebracht hatten, nun auch
anfingen, das politische Leben zu durchdringen —
FORTLAGE, *Allg. Monatschrift,* 1853, 777. Wir
Slawen wissen, dass die Geister einzelner Menschen
und ganzer Volker sich nur durch die Stufe ihrer
Entwicklung unterscheiden —MICKIEWICZ, *Slawische
Literatur,* II. 436. Le progrès ne disparait jamais,
mais il se déplace souvent. Il va des gouvernants
aux gouvernés. La tendance des révolutions est de
le ramener toujours parmi les gouvernants. Lorsqu'il
est à la tête des sociétés, il marche hardiment, car il
conduit. Lorsqu'il est dans la masse, il marche à
pas lents, car il lutte.—NAPOLEON III., *Des Idées
Napoléoniennes.* La loi du progrès avait jadis
l'inexorable rigueur du destin , elle prend maintenant
de jour en jour la douce puissance de la Providence.
C'est l'erreur, c'est l'iniquité, c'est le vice, que la
civilisation tend à emporter dans sa marche irrésis-
tible , mais la vie des individus et des peuples est
devenue pour elle une chose sacrée. Elle transforme
plutôt qu'elle ne détruit les choses qui s'opposent à
son développement ; elle procède par absorption
graduelle plutôt que par brusque exécution , elle aime

à conquérir par l'influence des idées plutôt que par la force des armes, un peuple, une classe, une institution qui résiste au progrès —VACHEROT, *Essais de Philosophie Critique*, 443. Peu à peu l'homme intellectuel finit par effacer l'homme physique — QUETELEʏ, *De l'Homme*, ıı 285 In dem Fortschritt der ethischen Anschauungen liegt daher der Kern des geschichtlichen Fortschritts uberhaupt —SCHAFER, *Arbeitsgebiet der Geschichte*, 24 Si l'homme a plus de devoirs à mesure qu'il avance en âge, ce qui est mélancolique, mais ce qui est vrai, de même aussi l'humanité est tenue d'avoir une morale plus sévère à mesure qu'elle prend plus de siècles —FAGUET, *Revue des Deux Mondes*, 1894, ııı. 871. Si donc il y a une loi de progrès, elle se confond avec la loi morale, et la condition fondamentale du progrès, c'est la pratique de cette loi —CARRAU, *Ib.*, 1875, v. 585. L'idée du progrès, du développement, me paraît être l'idée fondamentale contenue sous le mot de civilisation.— GUIZOT, *Cours d'Histoire*, 1828, 15. Le progrès n'est sous un autre nom, que la liberté en action.—BROGLIE, *Journal des Débats*, January 28, 1869. Le progrès social est continu. Il a ses périodes de fièvre ou d'atonie, de surexcitation ou de léthargie ; il a ses soubresauts et ses haltes, mais il avance toujours.— DE DECKER, *La Providence*, 174 Ce n'est pas au bonheur seul, c'est au perfectionnement que notre destin nous appelle , et la liberté politique est le plus puissant, le plus énergique moyen de perfectionnement que le ciel nous ait donné —B CONSTANT, *Cours de Politique*, ıı 559 To explode error, on

whichever side it lies, is certainly to secure progress.
—MARTINEAU, *Essays*, 1. 114. Die sämmtlichen
Freiheitsrechte, welche der heutigen Menschheit so
theuer sind, sind im Grunde nur Anwendungen des
Rechts der Entwickelung. — BLUNTSCHLI, *Kleine
Schriften*, 1. 51. Geistiges Leben ist auf Freiheit be-
ruhende Entwicklung, mit Freiheit vollzogene That und
geschichtlicher Fortschritt.—*Munchner Gel. Anzeigen*
1849, 11.83. Wie das Denken erst nach und nach reift, so
wird auch der freie Wille nicht fertig geboren, sondern
in der Entwickelung erworben.—TRENDELENBURG,
Logische Untersuchungen, 11. 94. Das Liberum Arbi-
trium im vollen Sinne (die vollständig aktuelle Macht
der Selbstbestimmung) lasst sich seinem Begriff
zufolge schlechterdings nicht unmittelbar geben ; es
kann nur erworben werden durch das Subjekt selbst,
in sich moralisch hervorgebracht werden kraft seiner
eigenen Entwickelung —ROTHE, *Ethik*, i 360 So
gewaltig sei der Andrang der Erfindungen und
Entdeckungen, dass " Entwicklungsperioden, die in
fruheren Zeiten erst in Jahrhunderten durchlaufen
wurden, die im Beginn unserer Zeitperiode noch der
Jahrzehnte bedurften, sich heute in Jahren vollenden,
haufig schon in voller Ausbildung ins Dasein treten "
—PHILIPPOVICH, *Fortschritt und Kulturentwicklung*,
1892, 1. quoting SIEMENS, 1886. Wir erkennen dass
dem Menschen die schwere korperliche Arbeit, von
der er in seinem Kampfe um's Dasein stets schwer
niedergedruckt war und grossenteils noch ist, mehr
und mehr durch die wachsende Benutzung der
Naturkrafte zur mechanischen Arbeitsleistung abge-

nommen wird, dass die ihm zufallende Arbeit immer
mehr eine intellektuelle wird.—SIEMENS, 1886, *Ib* 6.

[36] Once, however, he wrote —Darin konnte man
den idealen Kern der Geschichte des menschlichen
Geschlechtes uberhaupt sehen, dass in den Kampfen,
die sich in den gegenseitigen Interessen der Staaten
und Volker vollziehen, doch immer hohere Potenzen
emporkommen, die das Allgemeine demgemass um-
gestalten und ihm wieder einen anderen Charakter
verleihen.—RANKE, *Weltgeschichte*, iii. 1, 6

[37] Toujours et partout, les hommes furent de plus
en plus dominés par l'ensemble de leurs prédécesseurs,
dont ils purent seulement modifier l'empire nécessaire.
—COMTE, *Politique Positive*, iii. 621.

[38] La liberté est l'âme du commerce.—Il faut
laisser faire les hommes qui s'appliquent sans peine
à ce qui convient le mieux, c'est ce qui apporte le
plus d'avantage.—COLBERT, in *Comptes Rendus de
l'Institut*, xxxix 93

[39] Il n'y a que les choses humaines exposées dans
leur vérité, c'est-à-dire avec leur grandeur, leur
variété, leur inépuisable fécondité, qui aient le droit
de retenir le lecteur et qui le retiennent en effet.   Si
l'écrivain paraît une fois, il ennuie ou fait sourire de
pitié les lecteurs sérieux.—THIERS to STE. BEUVE,
Lundis, iii. 195.   Comme l'a dit Taine, la disparition
du style, c'est la perfection du style.—FAGUET, *Revue
Politique*, lii. 67.

[40] Ne m'applaudissez pas ; ce n'est pas moi qui
vous parle, c'est l'histoire qui parle par ma bouche
—*Revue Historique*, xli 278

[41] Das Evangelium trat als Geschichte in die Welt,
nicht als Dogma —wurde als Geschichte in der christlichen Kirche deponirt.—ROTHE, *Kirchengeschichte*,
ii. p x. Das Christenthum ist nicht der Herr
Christus, sondern dieser macht es. Es ist sein Werk,
und zwar ein Werk das er stets unter der Arbeit hat.—
Er selbst, Christus der Herr, bleibt der er ist in alle
Zukunft, dagegen liegt es ausdrucklich im Begriffe
seines Werks, des Christenthums, dass es nicht so bleibt
wie es anhebt.—ROTHE, *Allgemeine kirchliche Zeitschrift*, 1864, 299. Diess Werk, weil es dem Wesen
der Geschichte zufolge eine Entwickelung ist, muss
uber Stufen hinweggehen, die einander ablosen, und
von denen jede folgende neue immer nur unter der
Zertrummerung der ihr vorangehenden Platz greifen
kann —ROTHE, *Ib*. April 19, 1865. Je grosser ein
geschichtliches Princip ist, desto langsamer und uber
mehr Stufen hinweg entfaltet es seinen Gehalt , desto
langlebiger ist es aber ebendeshalb auch in diesen
seinen   unaufhorlichen   Abwandelungen.—ROTHE,
Stille Stunden, 301 Der christliche Glaube geht nicht
von der Anerkennung abstracter Lehrwahrheiten aus,
sondern von der Anerkennung einer Reihe von
Thatsachen, die in der Erscheinung Jesu ihren Mittel-
punkt haben.—NITZSCH, *Dogmengeschichte*, i. 17.
Der Gedankengang der evangelischen Erzahlung gibt
darum auch eine vollstandige Darstellung der christlichen Lehre in ihren wesentlichen Grundzugen ; aber
er gibt sie im allseitigen lebendigen Zusammenhange
mit der Geschichte der christlichen Offenbarung, und
nicht in einer theoretisch zusammenhangenden Folgen-

reihe von ethischen und dogmatischen Lehrsatzen.—
DEUTINGER, *Reich Gottes*, 1. p. v.

[42] L'Univers ne doit pas estre considéré seulement
dans ce qu'il est, pour le bien connoître, il faut le
voir aussi dans ce qu'il doit estre. C'est cet avenir
surtout qui a été le grand objet de Dieu dans la
création, et c'est pour cet avenir seul que le présent
existe.—D'HOUTEVILLE, *Essai sur la Providence*, 273
La Providence emploie les siècles à élever toujours un
plus grand nombre de familles et d'individus à ces
biens de la liberté et de l'égalité légitimes que, dans
l'enfance des sociétés, la force avait rendus le privilège
de quelques-uns.—GUIZOT, *Gouvernement de la France*,
1820, 9. La marche de la Providence n'est pas
assujettie à d'étroites limites, elle ne s'inquiète pas de
tirer aujourd'hui la conséquence du principe qu'elle a
posé hier ; elle la tirera dans des siècles, quand l'heure
sera venue, et pour raisonner lentement selon nous, sa
logique n'est pas moins sûre.—GUIZOT, *Histoire de la
Civilisation*, 20. Der Keim fortschreitender Entwicklung
ist, auch auf gottlichem Geheisse, der Menschheit
eingepflanzt. Die Weltgeschichte ist der blosse
Ausdruck einer vorbestimmten Entwicklung.—A.
HUMBOLDT, January 2, 1842, *Im Neuen Reich*, 1872,
1. 197. Das historisch grosse ist religios gross ; es ist
die Gottheit selbst, die sich offenbart.—RAUMER,
April 1807, *Erinnerungen*, 1. 85.

[43] Je suis arrivé à l'âge où je suis, à travers bien
des évènements différents, mais avec une seule cause,
celle de la liberté régulière —TOCQUEVILLE, May 1,
1852, *Œuvres Inédites*, 11. 185. Me trouvant dans un

pays où la religion et le libéralisme sont d'accord, j'avais respiré.—J'exprimais ce sentiment, il y a plus de vingt ans, dans l'avant-propos de la *Démocratie*. Je l'éprouve aujourd'hui aussi vivement que si j'étais encore jeune, et je ne sais s'il y a une seule pensée qui ait été plus constamment présente à mon esprit.— August 5, 1857, *Œuvres*, vi. 395. Il n'y a que la liberté (j'entends la modérée et la régulière) et la religion, qui, par un effort combiné, puissent soulever les hommes au-dessus du bourbier où l'égalité démo-cratique les plonge naturellement —December 1, 1852, *Œuvres*, vii. 295. L'un de mes rêves, le principal en entrant dans la vie politique, était de travailler à concilier l'esprit libéral et l'esprit de religion, la société nouvelle et l'église —November 15, 1843, *Œuvres Inédites*, ii. 121. La véritable grandeur de l'homme n'est que dans l'accord du sentiment libéral et du sentiment religieux.—September 17, 1853, *Œuvres Inédites*, ii. 228. Qui cherche dans la liberté autre chose qu'elle-même est fait pour servir.—*Ancien Régime*, 248. Je regarde, ainsi que je l'ai toujours fait, la liberté comme le premier des biens ; je vois toujours en elle l'une des sources les plus fécondes des vertus mâles et des actions grandes Il n'y a pas de tranquillité ni de bien-être qui puisse me tenir lieu d'elle.—January 7, 1856, *M*^{me} *Swetchine*, i. 452 La liberté a un faux air d'aristocratie, en donnant pleine carrière aux facultés humaines, en encou-rageant le travail et l'économie, elle fait ressortir les supériorités naturelles ou acquises —LABOULAYE, *L'É-tat et ses Limites*, 154 Dire que la liberté n'est point

H

par elle-même, qu'elle dépend d'une situation, d'une opportunité, c'est lui assigner une valeur négative. La liberté n'est pas dès qu'on la subordonne. Elle n'est pas un principe purement négatif, un simple élément de contrôle et de critique. Elle est le principe actif, créateur organisateur par excellence. Elle est le moteur et la règle, la source de toute vie, et le principe de l'ordre. Elle est, en un mot, le nom que prend la conscience souveraine, lorsque, se posant en face du monde social et politique, elle émerge du moi pour modeler les sociétés sur les données de la raison.— BRISSON, *Revue Nationale*, xxiii. 214. Le droit, dans l'histoire, est le développement progressif de la liberté, sous la loi de la raison.—LERMINIER, *Philosophie du Droit*, i. 211. En prouvant par les leçons de l'histoire que la liberté fait vivre les peuples et que le despotisme les tue, en montrant que l'expiation suit la faute et que la fortune finit d'ordinaire par se ranger du côté de la vertu, Montesquieu n'est ni moins moral ni moins religieux que Bossuet.—LABOU-LAYE, *Œuvres de Montesquieu*, ii. 109. Je ne comprendrais pas qu'une nation ne plaçât pas les libertés politiques au premier rang, parce que c'est des libertés politiques que doivent découler toutes les autres.— THIERS, *Discours*, x. 8, *March* 28, 1865. Nous sommes arrivés à une époque où la liberté est le but sérieux de tous, où le reste n'est plus qu'une question de moyens.—J. LEBEAU, *Observations sur le Pouvoir Royal* Liége, 1830, p. 10. Le libéralisme, ayant la prétention de se fonder uniquement sur les principes de la raison, croit d'ordinaire n'avoir pas besoin de tradition. Là est son erreur. L'erreur de l'école libérale est d'avoir trop cru qu'il est facile de créer la liberté par la réflexion, et de n'avoir pas vu qu'un établissement n'est solide que quand il a des racines historiques.—RENAN, 1858, *Nouvelle Revue*, lxxix. 596. Le respect des individus et des droits existants est autant au-dessus du bonheur de tous, qu'un intérêt moral surpasse un intérêt purement temporel. — RENAN, 1858, *Ib* lxxix. 597. Die Rechte gelten nichts, wo es sich handelt um das Recht, und das Recht der Freiheit kann nie verjahren, weil es die Quelle alles Rechtes selbst ist.—C. FRANTZ, *Ueber die Freiheit,* 110. Wir erfahren hicnieden nie die ganze Wahrheit : wir geniessen nie die ganze Freiheit.—REUSS, *Reden*, 56. Le gouvernement constitutionnel, comme tout gouvernement libre, présente et doit présenter un état de lutte permanent. La liberté est la perpétuité de la lutte —DE SERRE BROGLIE, *Nouvelles Études*, 243. The experiment of free government is not one which can be tried once for all. Every generation must try it for itself. As each new generation starts up to the responsibilities of manhood, there is, as it were, a new launch of Liberty, and its voyage of experiment begins afresh.—WINTHROP, *Addresses*, 163. L'histoire perd son véritable caractère du moment que la liberté en a disparu ; elle devient une sorte de physique sociale. C'est l'élément personnel de l'histoire qui en fait la réalité.—VACHEROT, *Revue des Deux Mondes*, 1869, IV 215. Demander la liberté pour soi et la refuser aux autres, c'est la définition

du despotisme.—LABOULAYE, December 4, 1874. Les
causes justes profitent de tout, des bonnes intentions
comme des mauvaises, des calculs personnels comme
des dévouemens courageux, de la démence, enfin,
comme de la raison —B. CONSTANT, *Les Cent Jours*,
ii. 29. Sie ist die Kunst, das Gute der schon weit
gediehenen Civilisation zu sichern.—BALTISCH, *Politische Freiheit*, 9. In einem Volke, welches sich zur
burgerlichen Gesellschaft, uberhaupt zum Bewusstseyn
der Unendlichkeit des Freien—entwickelt hat, ist
nur die constitutionelle Monarchie moglich.—HEGEL'S
Philosophie des Rechts, § 137, *Hegel und Preussen*,
1841, 31. Freiheit ist das hochste Gut. Alles
andere ist nur das Mittel dazu : gut falls es ein
Mittel dazu ist, ubel falls es dieselbe hemmt —
FICHTE. *Werke*, iv. 403. You are not to inquire
how your trade may be increased, nor how you are to
become a great and powerful people, but how your
liberties can be secured. For liberty ought to be the
direct end of your government.—PATRICK HENRY,
1788. WIRT, *Life of Henry*, 272.

⁴⁴ Historiæ ipsius præter delectationem utilitas
nulla est, quam ut religionis Christianæ veritas demon-
stretur, quod aliter quam per historiam fieri non
potest.—LEIBNIZ, *Opera*, ed. Dutens, vi. 297. The
study of Modern History is, next to Theology itself,
and only next in so far as Theology rests on a divine
revelation, the most thoroughly religious training that
the mind can receive It is no paradox to say that
Modern History, including Medieval History in the
term, is co extensive in its field of view, in its habits

of criticism, in the persons of its most famous students, with Ecclesiastical History.—STUBBS, *Lectures*,
9   Je regarde donc l'étude de l'histoire comme l'étude
de la providence.--L'histoire est vraiment une seconde
philosophie.—Si Dieu ne parle pas toujours, il agit
toujours en Dieu —D'AGUESSEAU, *Œuvres*, xv 34, 31,
35 Für diejenigen, welche das Wesen der menschlichen
Freiheit erkannt haben, bildet die denkende Betrachtung der Weltgeschichte, besonders des christlichen
Weltalters, die höchste, und umfassendste Theodicee.
—VATKE, *Die Menschliche Freiheit*, 1841, 516. La
théologie, que l'on regarde volontiers comme la plus
étroite et la plus stérile des sciences, en est, au contraire, la plus étendue et la plus féconde Elle confine
à toutes les études et touche à toutes les questions.
Elle renferme tous les éléments d'une instruction
libérale —SCHERER, *Mélanges*, 522 The belief that
the course of events and the agency of man are subject to the laws of a divine order, which it is alike
impossible for any one either fully to comprehend or
effectually to resist—this belief is the ground of all
our hope for the future destinies of mankind —
THIRLWALL, *Remains*, iii. 282. A true religion must
consist of ideas and facts both; not of ideas alone
without facts, for then it would be mere philosophy,
nor of facts alone without ideas, of which those facts
are the symbols, or out of which they are grounded,
for then it would be mere history.—COLERIDGE, *Table
Talk*, 144 It certainly appears strange that the men
most conversant with the order of the visible uni-
verse should soonest suspect it empty of directing

mind, and, on the other hand, that humanistic, moral
and historical studies—which first open the terrible
problems of suffering and grief, and contain all the
reputed provocatives of denial and despair—should
confirm, and enlarge rather than disturb, the prepossessions
of natural piety.—MARTINEAU, *Essays*, 1. 122.
Die Religion hat nur dann eine Bedeutung fur den
Menschen, wenn er in der Geschichte einen Punkt
findet, dem er sich vollig unbedingt hingeben kann.—
STEFFENS, *Christliche Religionsphilosophie*, 440, 1839.
Wir erkennen darin nur eine Thatigkeit des zu seinem
achten und wahren Leben, zu seinem verlornen,
objectiven Selbstverstandnisse sich zurucksehnenden
christlichen Geistes unserer Zeit, einen Ausdruck fur
das Bedurfniss desselben, sich aus den unwahren
und unachten Verkleidungen, womit ihn der moderne,
subjective Geschmack der letzten Entwicklungsphase
des theologischen Bewusstseyns umhullt hat, zu seiner
historischen allein wahren und ursprunglichen Gestalt
wiederzugebaren, zu derjenigen Bedeutung zuruckzu-
kehren, die ihm in dem Bewusstseyn der Geschichte
allein zukommt und deren Verstandniss in dem
wogenden luxuriosen Leben der modernen Theologie
langst untergegangen ist.—GEORGII, *Zeitschrift fur
Hist. Theologie*, ix. 5, 1839.

⁴⁵ Liberty, in fact, means just so far as it is realised,
the right man in the right place —SEELEY, *Lectures
and Essays*, 109

⁴⁶ In diesem Sinne ist Freiheit und sich entwickelnde
moralische Vernunft und Gewissen gleichbedeutend.
In diesem Sinne ist der Mensch frei, sobald sich das

Gewissen in ihm entwickelt —SCHEIDLER, *Ersch und Gruber*, xlix. 20. Aus der unendlichen und ewigen Geltung der menschlichen Personlichkeit vor Gott, aus der Vorstellung von der in Gott freien Personlichkeit, folgt auch der Anspruch auf das Recht derselben in der weltlichen Sphare, auf burgerliche und politische Freiheit, auf Gewissen und Religionsfreiheit, auf freie wissenschaftliche Forschung u s w., und namentlich die Forderung dass niemand lediglich zum Mittel fur andere diene.—MARTENSEN, *Christliche Ethik*, 1 50.

[47] Es giebt angeborne Menschenrechte, weil es angeborne Menschenpflichten giebt —WOLFF, *Naturrecht*, LŒPER, *Einleitung zu Faust*, lvii.

[48] La constitution de l'état reste jusqu'à un certain point à notre discrétion. La constitution de la société ne dépend pas de nous, elle est donnée par la force des choses, et si l'on veut élever le langage, elle est l'œuvre de la Providence.—RÉMUSAT, *Revue des Deux Mondes*, 1861, v. 795.

[49] Die Freiheit ist bekanntlich kein Geschenk der Gotter, sondern ein Gut das jedes Volk sich selbst verdankt und das nur bei dem erforderlichen Mass moralischer Kraft und Wurdigkeit gedeiht.—IHERING, *Geist des Romischen Rechts*, ii. 290. Liberty, in the very nature of it, absolutely requires and even supposes, that people be able to govern themselves in those respects in which they are free, otherwise their wickedness will be in proportion to their liberty, and this greatest of blessings will become a curse.— BUTLER, *Sermons*, 331. In each degree and each

variety of public development there are corresponding institutions, best answering the public needs, and
what is meat to one is poison to another. Freedom
is for those who are fit for it.—PARKMAN, *Canada*,
396. Die Freiheit ist die Wurzel einer neuen Schopfung in der Schopfung.—SEDERHOLM, *Die ewigen
Thatsachen*, 86.

[50] La liberté politique, qui n'est qu'une complexité
plus grande, de plus en plus grande, dans le gouvernement d'un peuple, à mesure que le peuple lui-même
contient un plus grand nombre de forces diverses
ayant droit et de vivre et de participer à la chose
publique, est un fait de civilisation qui s'impose lentement à une société organisée, mais qui n'apparaît point
comme un principe à une société qui s'organise.—
FAGUET, *Revue des Deux Mondes*, 1889, ii. 942.

[51] Il y a bien un droit du plus sage, mais non pas
un droit du plus fort.—La justice est le droit du plus
faible.—JOUBERT, *Pensées*, i. 355, 358.

[52] Nicht durch ein pflanzenahnliches Wachsthum,
nicht aus den dunklen Grunden der Volksempfindung,
sondern durch den mannlichen Willen, durch die
Ueberzeugung, durch die That, durch den Kampf
entsteht, behauptet, entwickelt sich das Recht. Sein
historisches Werden ist ein bewusstes, im hellen
Mittagslicht der Erkenntniss und der Gesetzgebung —
Rundschau, Nov. 1893, 313. Nicht das Normale,
Zahme, sondern das Abnorme, Wilde, bildet uberall die
Grundlage und den Anfang einer neuen Ordnung —
LASAULX, *Philosophie der Geschichte*, 143

[53] Um den Sieg zu vervollstandigen, erubrigte das

zweite Stadium oder die Aufgabe die Berechtigung
der Mehrheit nach allen Seiten hin zur gleichen
Berechtigung aller zu erweitern, d.h bis zur Gleichstel-
lung aller Bekenntnisse im Kirchenrecht, aller Volker
im Volkerrecht, aller Staatsburger im Staatsrecht und
aller socialen Interessen im Gesellschaftsrecht fortzu-
fuhren.—A. SCHMIDT, *Zuricher Monatschrift*, i. 68

[54] Notre histoire ne nous enseignait nullement la
liberté Le jour où la France voulut être libre, elle
eut tout à créer, tout à inventer dans cet ordre de
faits.—Cependant il faut marcher, l'avenir appelle les
peuples. Quand on n'a point pour cela l'impulsion
du passé, il faut bien se confier à la raison.—DUPONT
WHITE, *Revue des Deux Mondes*, 1861, vi. 191. Le
peuple français a peu de goût pour le développement
graduel des institutions. Il ignore son histoire, il
ne s'y reconnaît pas, elle n'a pas laissé de trace dans
sa conscience —SCHERER, *Études Critiques*, i. 100
Durch die Revolution befreiten sich die Franzosen
von ihrer Geschichte.—ROSENKRANZ, *Aus einem
Tagebuch*, 199

[55] The discovery of the comparative method in
philology, in mythology—let me add in politics and
history and the whole range of human thought—marks
a stage in the progress of the human mind at least
as great and memorable as the revival of Greek and
Latin learning —FREEMAN, *Historical Essays*, iv. 301.
The diffusion of a critical spirit in history and literature
is affecting the criticism of the Bible in our own day
in a manner not unlike the burst of intellectual life in
the fifteenth and sixteenth centuries.—JOWETT, *Essays*

and Reviews, 346. As the revival of literatuie in the sixteenth century produced the Reformation, so the growth of the critical spirit, and the change that has come over mental science, and the mere increase of knowledge of all kinds, threaten now a revolution less external but not less profound.—HADDAN, *Replies*, 348.

[50] In his just contempt and detestation of the crimes and follies of the Revolutionists, he suffers himself to forget that the revolution itself is a process of the Divine Providence, and that as the folly of men is the wisdom of God, so are their iniquities instruments of His goodness.—COLERIDGE, *Biographia Literaria*, ii. 240. In other parts of the world, the idea of revolutions in government is, by a mournful and indissoluble association, connected with the idea of wars, and all the calamities attendant on wars. But happy experience teaches us to view such revolutions in a very different light—to consider them only as progressive steps in improving the knowledge of government, and increasing the happiness of society and mankind.—J WILSON, November 26, 1787, *Works*, iii. 293. La Révolution, c'est-à-dire l'œuvre des siècles, ou, si vous voulez, le renouvellement progressif de la société, ou encore, sa nouvelle constitution.—RÉMUSAT, *Correspondance*, October 11, 1818. A ses yeux loin d'avoir rompu le cours naturel des évènements, ni la Révolution d'Angleterre, ni la nôtre, n'ont rien dit, rien fait, qui n'eût été dit, souhaité, fait, ou tenté cent fois avant leur explosion. " Il faut en ceci," dit-il, "tout accorder à leurs adversaires, les sur-

passer même en sévérité, ne regarder à leurs accusations
que pour y ajouter, s'ils en oublient , et puis les sommer
de dresser, à leur tour, le compte des erreurs, des crimes,
et des maux de ces temps et de ces pouvoirs qu'ils ont
pris sous leur garde "—*Revue de Paris*, xvi. 303, on
Guizot. Quant aux nouveautés mises en œuvre par
la Révolution Française on les retrouve une à une,
en remontant d'âge en âge, chez les philosophes du
XVIIIe siècle, chez les grands penseurs du XVIe, chez
certains Pères d'Église et jusque dans la République de
Platon —En présence de cette belle continuité de
l'histoire, qui ne fait pas plus de sauts que la nature,
devant cette solidarité nécessaire des révolutions avec
le passé qu'elles brisent —KRANTZ, *Revue Politique*,
xxxiii 264 L'esprit du XIXe siècle est de comprendre et
de juger les choses du passé. Notre œuvre est d'expliquer ce que le XVIIIe siècle avait mission de nier.
—VACHEROT, *De la Démocratie*, pref , 28.

[57] La commission recherchera, dans toutes les parties
des archives pontificales, les pièces relatives à l'abus
que les papes ont fait de leur ministère spirituel contre
l'autorité des souverains et la tranquillité des peuples.
—DAUNOU, *Instructions*, Jan. 3, 1811. LABORDE,
Inventaires, p. cxii.

[58] Aucun des historiens remarquables de cette
époque n'avait senti encore le besoin de chercher les
faits hors des livres imprimés, aux sources primitives,
la plupart inédites alors, aux manuscrits de nos
bibliothèques, aux documents de nos archives.—
MICHELET, *Histoire de France*, 1869, 1 2

[59] Doch besteht eine Grenze, wo die Geschichte

aufhort und das Archiv anfangt, und die von der
Geschichtschreibung nicht uberschritten werden sollte.
Unsere Zeit, 1866, ii. 635. Il faut avertir nos jeunes
historiens à la fois de la nécessité inéluctable du
document et, d'autre part, du danger qu'il présente —
M HANOTAUX

[60] This process consists in determining with documentary proofs, and by minute investigations duly set
forth, the literal, precise, and positive inferences to
be drawn at the present day from every authentic
statement, without regard to commonly received
notions, to sweeping generalities, or to possible consequences.—HARRISSE, *Discovery of America*, 1892,
p vi Perhaps the time has not yet come for synthetic
labours in the sphere of History It may be that the
student of the Past must still content himself with critical inquiries.—*Ib*. p. v. Few scholars are critics, few
critics are philosophers, and few philosophers look with
equal care on both sides of a question —W. S. LANDOR
in HOLYOAKE'S *Agitator's Life*, ii. 15. Introduire dans
l'histoire, et sans tenir compte des passions politiques
et religieuses, le doute méthodique que Descartes, le
premier, appliqua à l'étude de la philosophie, n'est-ce
pas là une excellente méthode ? n'est-ce pas même
la meilleure ?—CHANTELAUZE, *Correspondant*, 1883, i.
129 La critique historique ne sera jamais populaire.
Comme elle est de toutes les sciences la plus délicate,
la plus déliée, elle n'a de crédit qu'auprès des esprits
cultivés —CHERBULIEZ, *Revue des Deux Mondes*, xcvii.
517 Nun liefert aber die Kritik, wenn sie rechter
Art ist, immer nur einzelne Data, gleichsam die Atome

des Thatbestandes, und jede Kombination, jede Zu-
sammenfassung und Schlussfolgerung, ohne die es
doch einmal nicht abgeht, ist ein subjektiver Akt des
Forschers. Demnach blieb Waitz, bei der eigenen
Arbeit wie bei jener der anderen, immer hochst mis-
trauisch gegen jedes Résumé, jede Definition, jedes
abschliessende Wort —SYBEL, *Historische Zeitschrift*,
lvi 484. Mit blosser Kritik wird darin nichts aus-
gerichtet, denn die ist nur eine Vorarbeit, welche da
aufhort wo die echte historische Kunst anfangt.—
LASAULX, *Philosophie der Kunste*, 212.

[61] The only case in which such extraneous matters
can be fairly called in is when facts are stated resting
on testimony; then it is not only just, but it is
necessary for the sake of truth, to inquire into the
habits of mind of him by whom they are adduced
—BABBAGE, *Bridgewater Treatise*, p. xiv.

[62] There is no part of our knowledge which it is
more useful to obtain at first hand—to go to the
fountain-head for—than our knowledge of History.—
J. S. MILL, *Inaugural Address*, 34. The only sound
intellects are those which, in the first instance, set their
standard of proof high.—J. S. MILL, *Examination of
Hamilton's Philosophy*, 525.

[63] There are so few men mentally capable of seeing
both sides of a question; so few with consciences
sensitively alive to the obligation of seeing both sides,
so few placed under conditions either of circumstance
or temper, which admit of their seeing both sides.—
GREG, *Political Problems*, 1870, 173. Il n'y a que les
Allemands qui sachent être aussi complètement objec-

tifs. Ils se dédoublent, pour ainsi dire, en deux hommes,
l'un qui a des principes très arrêtés et des passions très
vives, l'autre qui sait voir et observer comme s'il n'en
avait point.—LAVELEYE, *Revue des Deux Mondes*, 1868,
i. 431. L'écrivain qui penche trop dans le sens où
il incline, et qui ne se défie pas de ses qualités
presque autant que ses défauts, cet écrivain tourne à la
manière.—SCHERER, *Mélanges*, 484. Il faut faire volte-
face, et vivement, franchement, tourner le dos au
moyen âge, à ce passé morbide, qui, même quand il
n'agit pas, influe terriblement par la contagion de la
mort. Il ne faut ni combattre, ni critiquer, mais
oublier. Oublions et marchons !—MICHELET, *La
Bible de l'Humanité*, 483. It has excited surprise
that Thucydides should speak of Antiphon, the traitor
to the democracy, and the employer of assassins, as "a
man inferior in virtue to none of his contemporaries."
But neither here nor elsewhere does Thucydides pass
moral judgments.—JOWETT, *Thucydides*, ii. 501.

[64] Non theologi provinciam suscepimus ; scimus
enim quantum hoc ingenii nostri tenuitatem superet ·
ideo sufficit nobis τὸ ὅτι fideliter ex antiquis auctoribus
retulisse.—MORINUS, *De Pœnitentia*, ix. 10.—Il
faut avouer que la religion chrétienne a quelque chose
d'étonnant ! C'est parce que vous y êtes né, dira-t-
on. Tant s'en faut, je me roidis contre par cette
raison-là même, de peur que cette prévention ne me
suborne.—PASCAL, *Pensées*, XVI, 7.—I was fond of
Fleury for a reason which I express in the advertise-
ment , because it presented a sort of photograph of
ecclesiastical history without any comment upon it

In the event, that simple representation of the early
centuries had a good deal to do with unsettling me.—
NEWMAN, *Apologia*, 152.—Nur was sich vor dem
Richterstuhl einer achten, unbefangenen, nicht durch
die Brille einer philosophischen oder dogmatischen
Schule stehenden Wissenschaft als wahr bewahrt, kann
zur Erbauung, Belehrung und Warnung tuchtig seyn.
—NEANDER, *Kirchengeschichte*, i. p. vii.   Wie weit bei
katholischen Publicisten bei der Annahme der Ansicht
von der Staatsanstalt apologetische Gesichtspunkte
massgebend gewesen sind, mag dahingestellt bleiben.
Der Historiker darf sich jedoch nie durch apologetische Zwecke leiten lassen ; sein einziges Ziel soll
die Ergrundung der Wahrheit sein.- -PASTOR, *Geschichte
der Pabste*, ii. 545.   Church history falsely written is
a school of vainglory, hatred, and uncharitableness ;
truly written, it is a discipline of humility, of charity,
of mutual love.—SIR W. HAMILTON, *Discussions*, 506.
The more trophies and crowns of honour the Church
of former ages can be shown to have won in the ser-
vice of her adorable head, the more tokens her history
can be brought to furnish of his powerful presence in
her midst, the more will we be pleased and rejoice,
Protestant though we be —NEVIN, *Mercersburg Review*,
1851, 168.   S'il est une chose à laquelle j'ai donné
tous mes soins, c'est à ne pas laisser influencer mes
jugements par les opinions politiques ou religieuses ,
que si j'ai quelquefois péché par quelque excès, c'est
par la bienveillance pour les œuvres de ceux qui
pensent autrement que moi.—MONOD, *R. Hist* , xvi.
184.   Nous n'avons nul intérêt à faire parler l'histoire

en faveur de nos propres opinions. C'est son droit imprescriptible que le narrateur reproduise tous les faits sans aucune réticence et range toutes les évolutions dans leur ordre naturel. Notre récit restera complètement en dehors des préoccupations de la dogmatique et des déclamations de la polémique. Plus les questions auxquelles nous aurons à toucher agitent et passionnent de nos jours les esprits, plus il est du devoir de l'historien de s'effacer devant les faits qu'il veut faire connaître —REUSS, *Nouvelle Revue de Théologie*, vi. 193, 1860 To love truth for truth's sake is the principal part of human perfection in this world, and the seed plot of all other virtues.—LOCKE, *Letter to Collins.* Il n'est plus possible aujourd'hui à l'historien d'être national dans le sens étroit du mot. Son patriotisme à lui c'est l'amour de la vérité. Il n'est pas l'homme d'une race ou d'un pays, il est l'homme de tous les pays, il parle au nom de la civilisation générale. —LANFREY, *Hist de Nap.*, iii. 2, 1870. Juger avec les parties de soi-même qui sont le moins des formes du tempérament, et le plus des facultés pénétrées et modelées par l'expérience, par l'étude, par l'investigation, par le non-moi.—FAGUET, *R. de Paris*, i 151. Aucun critique n'est aussi impersonnel que lui, aussi libre de parti pris et d'opinions préconçues, aussi objectif.— Il ne mêle ou paraît mêler à ses appréciations ni inclinations personnelles de goût ou d'humeur, ou théories d'aucune sorte.—G. MONOD, of Faguet, *Revue Historique*, xlii. 417. On dirait qu'il a peur, en généralisant ses observations, en systématisant ses connaissances, de mêler de lui-même aux choses —Je lis tout un volume

de M. Faguet, sans penser une fois à M. Faguet. je
ne vois que les originaux qu'il montre.—J'envisage
toujours une réalité objective, jamais l'idée de M.
Faguet, jamais la doctrine de M. Faguet.— LANSON,
Revue Politique, 1894, i. 98.

[65] It should teach us to disentangle principles first
from parties, and again from one another, first of all
as showing how imperfectly all parties represent their
own principles, and then how the principles themselves are a mingled tissue.—ARNOLD, *Modern History*, 184. I find it a good rule, when I am con-
templating a person from whom I want to learn,
always to look out for his strength, being confident
that the weakness will discover itself —MAURICE,
Essays, 305. We may seek for agreement some-
where with our neighbours, using that as a point of
departure for the sake of argument. It is this latter
course that I wish here to explain and defend. The
method is simple enough, though not yet very familiar.
—It aims at conciliation, it proceeds by making the
best of our opponent's case, instead of taking him at
his worst.—The most interesting part of every disputed
question only begins to appear when the rival ideals
admit each other's right to exist.—A. SIDGWICK,*Distinc-
tion and the Criticism of Beliefs*, 1892, 211. That cruel
reticence in the breasts of wise men which makes them
always hide their deeper thought.—RUSKIN,*Sesame and
Lilies*, i. 16. Je offener wir die einzelnen Wahrheiten
des Sozialismus anerkennen, desto erfolgreicher konnen
wir seine fundamentalen Unwahrheiten widerlegen —
ROSCHER, *Deutsche Vierteljahrschrift*, 1849, 1 177.

I

[66] Dann habe ihn die Wahrnehmung, dass manche Angaben in den historischen Romanen Walter Scott's, mit den gleichzeitigen Quellen im Widerspruch standen, "mit Erstaunen" erfüllt, und ihn zu dem Entschlusse gebracht, auf das Gewissenhafteste an der Ueberlieferung der Quellen festzuhalten —SYBEL, *Gedachtnissrede auf Ranke Akad. der Wissenschaften*, 1887, p. 6. Sich frei zu halten von allem Widerschein der Gegenwart, sogar, soweit das menschenmoglich, von dem der eignen subjectiven Meinung in den Dingen des Staates, der Kirche und der Gesellschaft —A. DOVE, *Im Neuen Reich*, 1875, ii. 967. Wir sind durchaus nicht fur die leblose und schemenartige Darstellungsweise der Ranke'schen Schule eingenommen; es wird uns immer kuhl bis ans Herz heran, wenn wir derartige Schilderungen der Reformation und der Revolution lesen, welche so ganz im kuhlen Element des Pragmatismus sich bewegen und dabei so ganz Undinenhaft sind und keine Seele haben.—Wir lassen es uns lieber gefallen, dass die Manner der Geschichte hier und dort gehofmeistert werden, als dass sie uns mit Glasaugen ansehen, so meisterhaft immer die Kunst sein mag die sie ihnen eingesetzt hat.—GOTTSCHALL, *Unsere Zeit*, 1866, ii. 636, 637. A vivre avec des diplomates, il leur a pris des qualités qui sont un défaut chez un historien. L'historien n'est pas un témoin, c'est un juge; c'est à lui d'accuser et de condamner au nom du passé opprimé et dans l'intérêt de l'avenir —LABOULAYE on RANKE. *Débats*, January 12, 1852.

[67] Un théologien qui a composé une éloquente
histoire de la Réformation, rencontrant à Berlin un
illustre historien qui, lui aussi, a raconté Luther et le
XVIe siècle, l'embrassa avec effusion en le traitant
de confrère. "Ah! permettez," lui répondit l'autre
en se dégageant, "il y a une grande différence entre
nous : vous êtes avant tout chrétien, et je suis avant
tout historien."—CHERBULIEZ, *Revue des Deux Mondes*,
1872, i. 537.

[68] Nackte Wahrheit ohne allen Schmuck, grundliche
Erforschung des Einzelnen; das Uebrige, Gott befohlen.
—*Werke*, xxxiv. 24. Ce ne sont pas les théories qui
doivent nous servir de base dans la recherche des
faits, mais ce sont les faits qui doivent nous servir de
base pour la composition des théories.—VINCENT,
Nouvelle Revue de Théologie, 1859, ii. 252.

[69] Die zwanglose Anordnungs—die leichte und
leise Andeutungskunst des grossen Historikers voll
zu wurdigen, hinderte ihn in fruherer Zeit sein
Bedurfniss nach scharfer begrifflicher Ordnung und
Ausfuhrung, spater, und in immer zunehmenden
Grade, sein Sinn fur strenge Sachlichkeit, und genaue
Erforschung der ursachlichen Zusammenhange, noch
mehr aber regte sich seine geradherzige Offenheit
seine mannliche Ehrlichkeit, wenn er hinter den fein
verstrichenen Farben der Rankeschen Erzahlungs-
bilder die gedeckte Haltung des klugen Diplomaten
zu entdecken glaubte.—HAYM, *Duncker's Leben*, 437.
The ground of criticism is indeed, in my opinion,
nothing else but distinct attention, which every reader
should endeavour to be master of.—HARE, *Dec.*, 1736,

Warburton's Works, xiv. 98. Wenn die Quellenkritik so verstanden wird, als sei sie der Nachweis, wie ein Autor den andern benutzt hat, so ist das nur ein gelegentliches Mittel — eins unter anderen — ihre Aufgabe, den Nachweis der Richtigkeit zu losen oder vorzubereiten.—DROYSEN, *Historik*, 18.

[70] L'esprit scientifique n'est autre en soi que l'instinct du travail et de la patience, le sentiment de l'ordre, de la réalité et de la mesure.—PAPILLON, *R. des Deux Mondes*, 1873, v. 704. Non seulement les sciences, mais toutes les institutions humaines s'organisent de même, et sous l'empire des mêmes idées régulatrices —COURNOT, *Idées Fondamentales*, i. 4. There is no branch of human work whose constant laws have not close analogy with those which govern every other mode of man's exertion. But more than this, exactly as we reduce to greater simplicity and surety any one group of these practical laws, we shall find them passing the mere condition of connection or analogy, and becoming the actual expression of some ultimate nerve or fibre of the mighty laws which govern the moral world.—RUSKIN, *Seven Lamps*, 4. The sum total of all intellectual excellence is good sense and method When these have passed into the instinctive readiness of habit, when the wheel revolves so rapidly that we cannot see it revolve at all, then we call the combination genius. But in all modes alike, and in all professions, the two sole component parts, even of genius, are good sense and method.—COLE-RIDGE, *June*, 1814, *Mem. of Coleorton*, ii. 172. Si l'exercice d'un art nous empêche d'en apprendre un

autre, il n'en est pas ainsi dans les sciences . la connoissance d'une vérité nous aide à en decouvrir une
autre.—Toutes les sciences sont tellement liées
ensemble qu'il est bien plus facile de les apprendre
toutes à la fois que d'en apprendre une seule en la
détachant des autres.—Il ne doit songer qu'à augmenter
les lumières naturelles de sa raison, non pour résoudre
telle ou telle difficulté de l'école, mais pour que dans
chaque circonstance de la vie son intelligence montre
d'avance à sa volonté le parti qu'elle doit prendre.—
DESCARTES, *Œuvres Choisies*, 300, 301. *Règles pour
la Direction de l'Esprit.* La connaissance de la méthode
qui a guidé l'homme de génie n'est pas moins utile au
progrès de la science et même à sa propre gloire, que
ses découvertes.—LAPLACE, *Système du Monde*, ii. 371
On ne fait rien sans idées préconçues, il faut avoir
seulement la sagesse de ne croire à leurs déductions
qu'autant que l'expérience les confirme. Les idées
préconçues, soumises au contrôle sévère de l'expéri-
mentation, sont la flamme vivante des sciences d'observation ; les idées fixes en sont le danger —PASTEUR,
in *Histoire d'un Savant*, 284. Douter des vérités
humaines, c'est ouvrir la porte aux découvertes ; en
faire des articles de foi, c'est la fermer.—DUMAS,
Discours, i. 123.

[71] We should not only become familiar with the laws
of phenomena within our own pursuit, but also with
the modes of thought of men engaged in other discussions and researches, and even with the laws of
knowledge itself, that highest philosophy.—Above all
things, know that we call you not here to run your minds

into our moulds. We call you here on an excursion, on an adventure, on a voyage of discovery into space as yet uncharted.—ALLBUTT, *Introductory Address at St. George's*, October 1889. Consistency in regard to opinions is the slow poison of intellectual life.—DAVY, *Memoirs*, 68.

[72] Ce sont vous autres physiologistes des corps vivants, qui avez appris à nous autres physiologistes de la société (qui est aussi un corps vivant) la manière de l'observer et de tirer des conséquences de nos observations.—J. B. SAY to DE CANDOLLE, June 1, 1827.—DE CANDOLLE, *Mémoires*, 567.

[73] Success is certain to the pure and true : success to falsehood and corruption, tyranny and aggression, is only the prelude to a greater and an irremediable fall.—STUBBS, *Seventeen Lectures*, 20. The Carlylean faith, that the cause we fight for, so far as it is true, is sure of victory, is the necessary basis of all effective activity for good.—CAIRD, *Evolution of Religion*, ii. 43. It is the property of truth to be fearless, and to prove victorious over every adversary. Sound reasoning and truth, when adequately communicated, must always be victorious over error.—GODWIN, *Political Justice* (Conclusion) Vice was obliged to retire and give place to virtue. This will always be the consequence when truth has fair play. Falsehood only dreads the attack, and cries out for auxiliaries. Truth never fears the encounter ; she scorns the aid of the secular arm, and triumphs by her natural strength.—FRANKLIN, *Works*, 11. 292. It is a condition of our race that we must ever wade through error in our advance

towards truth . and it may even be said that in many cases we exhaust almost every variety of error before we attain the desired goal.—BABBAGE, *Bridgewater Treatise*, 27. Les hommes ne peuvent, en quelque genre que ce soit, arriver à quelque chose de raisonnable qu'après avoir, en ce même genre, épuisé toutes les sottises imaginables. Que de sottises ne dirions-nous pas maintenant, si les anciens ne les avaient pas déjà dites avant nous, et ne nous les avaient, pour ainsi dire, enlevées !—FONTENELLE. Without premature generalisations the true generalisation would never be arrived at.—H. SPENCER, *Essays*, ii. 57. The more important the subject of difference, the greater, not the less, will be the indulgence of him who has learned to trace the sources of human error,— of error, that has its origin not in our weakness and imperfection merely, but often in the most virtuous affections of the heart.—BROWN, *Philosophy of the Human Mind*, i. 48, 1824. Parmi les châtiments du crime qui ne lui manquent jamais, à côté de celui que lui inflige la conscience, l'histoire lui en inflige un autre encore, éclatant et manifeste, l'impuissance.— COUSIN, *Phil Mod*. ii 24. L'avenir de la science est garanti ; car dans le grand livre scientifique tout s'ajoute et rien ne se perd. L'erreur ne fonde pas , aucune erreur ne dure très longtemps.—RENAN, *Feuilles Détachées*, xiii. Toutes les fois que deux hommes sont d'un avis contraire sur la même chose, à coup sûr, l'un ou l'autre se trompe , bien plus, aucun ne semble posséder la vérité ; car si les raisons de l'un étoient certaines et évidentes, il pourroit les exposer à l'autre de telle manière qu'il finiroit par le convaincre également.—DESCARTES, *Règles Œuvres Choisies*, 302. Le premier principe de la critique est qu'une doctrine ne captive ses adhérents que par ce qu'elle a de légitime —RENAN, *Essais de Morale*, 184. Was dem Wahn solche Macht giebt ist wirklich nicht er selbst, sondern die ihm zu Grunde liegende und darin nur verzerrte Wahrheit.—FRANTZ, *Schelling's Philosophie*, 1. 62. Quand les hommes ont vu une fois la vérité dans son éclat, ils ne peuvent plus l'oublier. Elle reste debout, et tôt ou tard elle triomphe, parce qu'elle est la pensée de Dieu et le besoin du monde. —MIGNET, *Portraits*, II 295. C'est toujours le sens commun inaperçu qui fait la fortune des hypothèses auxquelles il se mêle —COUSIN, *Fragments Phil.* i. 51. Preface of 1826. Wer da sieht wie der Irrthum selbst ein Träger mannigfaltigen und bleibenden Fortschritts wird, der wird auch nicht so leicht aus dem thatsachlichen Fortschritt der Gegenwart auf Unumstosslichkeit unserer Hypothesen schliessen.—Das richtigste Resultat der geschichtlichen Betrachtung ist die akademische Ruhe, mit welcher unsere Hypothesen und Theorieen ohne Feindschaft und ohne Glauben als das betrachtet werden was sie sind; als Stufen in jener unendlichen Annäherung an die Wahrheit, welche die Bestimmung unserer intellectuellen Entwickelung zu sein scheint —LANGE, *Geschichte des Materialismus*, 502, 503. Hominum errores divina providentia reguntur, ita ut sæpe male jacta bene cadant —LEIBNIZ, ed. Klopp, i., p. lii. Sainte-Beuve n'était même pas de la race des libéraux, c'est-à-dire de ceux qui croient que, tout compte fait, et dans un état de civilisation donné, le bien triomphe du mal à armes égales, et la vérité de l'erreur.—D'HAUSSONVILLE, *Revue des Deux Mondes*, 1875, i. 567.   In the progress of the human mind, a period of controversy amongst the cultivators of any branch of science must necessarily precede the period of unanimity.—TORRENS, *Essay on the Production of Wealth*, 1821, p. xiii.   Even the spread of an error is part of the wide-world process by which we stumble into mere approximations to truth.—L. STEPHEN, *Apology of an Agnostic*, 81   Errors, to be dangerous, must have a great deal of truth mingled with them ; it is only from this alliance that they can ever obtain an extensive circulation.—S. SMITH, *Moral Philosophy*, 7.   The admission of the few errors of Newton himself is at least of as much importance to his followers in science as the history of the progress of his real discoveries.—YOUNG, *Works*, iii. 621.   Error is almost always partial truth, and so consists in the exaggeration or distortion of one verity by the suppression of another, which qualifies and modifies the former.— MIVART, *Genesis of Species*, 3.   The attainment of scientific truth has been effected, to a great extent, by the help of scientific errors.—HUXLEY : WARD, *Reign of Victoria*, ii. 337.   Jede neue tief eingreifende Wahrheit hat meiner Ansicht nach erst das Stadium der Einseitigkeit durchzumachen.—IHERING, *Geist des R. Rechts*, ii. 22.   The more readily we admit the possibility of our own cherished convictions being mixed with error, the more vital and helpful whatever is right in them will become.—RUSKIN, *Ethics of the Dust*, 225. They hardly grasp the plain truth unless they examine the error which it cancels.—CORY, *Modern English History*, 1880, i. 109   Nur durch Irrthum kommen wir, der eine kurzeren und glucklicheren Schrittes, als der andere, zur Wahrheit, und die Geschichte darf nirgends diese Verirrungen ubergehen, wenn sie Lehrerin und Warnerin fur die nachfolgenden Geschlechter werden will.—*Munchen Gel. Anzeigen*, 1840, i. 737.

[74] Wie die Weltgeschichte das Weltgericht ist, so kann in noch allgemeinerem Sinne gesagt werden, dass das gerechte Gericht, d.h. die wahre Kritik einer Sache, nur in ihrer Geschichte liegen kann   Insbesondere in der Hinsicht lehrt die Geschichte denjenigen, der ihr folgt, ihre eigene Methode, dass ihr Fortschritt niemals ein reines Vernichten, sondern nur ein Aufheben im philosophischen Sinne ist.—STRAUSS, *Hallische Jahrbucher*, 1839, 120.

[75] Dans tous les livres qu'il lit, et il en dévore des quantités, Darwin ne note que les passages qui contrarient ses idées systématiques.—Il collectionne les difficultés, les cas épineux, les critiques possibles.—VERNIER, *Le Temps*, 6 Décembre, 1887.   Je demandais à un savant célèbre où il en était de ses recherches. "Cela ne marche plus," me dit-il, "je ne trouve plus de faits contradictoires." Ainsi le savant cherche à se contredire lui-même pour faire avancer sa pensée.—JANET, *Journal des Savants*, 1892, 20.   Ein Umstand, der uns die Selbstandigkeit des Ganges der Wissenschaft anschaulich machen kann, ist auch der. dass

der Irrthum, wenn er nur grundlich behandelt wird,
fast ebenso fordernd ist als das Finden der Wahrheit,
denn er erzeugt fortgesetzten Widerspruch.—BAER,
Blicke auf die Entwicklung der Wissenschaft, 120. It
is only by virtue of the opposition which it has sur-
mounted that any truth can stand in the human mind.—
BISHOP TEMPLE , KINGLAKE, *Crimea*, *Winter Troubles*,
app. 104. I have for many years found it expedient
to lay down a rule for my own practice, to confine my
reading mainly to those journals the general line of
opinions in which is adverse to my own.—HARE,
Means of Unity, i. 19. Kant had a harder struggle
with himself than he could possibly have had with any
critic or opponent of his philosophy —CAIRD, *Philosophy of Kant*, 1889, i. p. ix.

[76] The social body is no more liable to arbitrary
changes than the individual body.—A full perception
of the truth that society is not a mere aggregate, but
an organic growth, that it forms a whole the laws of
whose growth can be studied apart from those of the
individual atom, supplies the most characteristic pos-
tulate of modern speculation.—L. STEPHEN, *Science of
Ethics*, 31. Wie in dem Leben des Einzelnen Menschen kein Augenblick eines vollkommenen Stillstandes
wahrgenommen wird, sondern stete organische Entwicklung, so verhalt es sich auch in dem Leben
der Volker, und in jedem einzelnen Element, woraus
dieses Gesammtleben besteht. So finden wir in der
Sprache stete Fortbildung und Entwicklung, und auf
gleiche Weise in dem Recht. Und auch diese
Fortbildung steht unter demselben Gesetz der

Erzeugung aus innerer Kraft und Nothwendigkeit, unabhangig von Zufall und individueller Willkur, wie die ursprungliche Entstehung.—SAVIGNY, *System*, i. 16, 17. Seine eigene Entdeckung, dass auch die geistige Produktion, bis ·in einem gewissen Punkte wenigstens, unter dem Gesetze der Kausalitat steht, dass jedeiner nur geben kann was er hat, nur hat was er irgendwoher bekommen, muss auch fur ihn selber gelten.—BEKKER, *Das Recht des Besitzes bei den Romern*, 3, 1880. Die geschichtliche Wandlung des Rechts, in welcher vergangene Jahrhunderte halb ein Spiel des Zufalls und halb ein Werk vernunftelnder Willkur sahen, als gesetzmassige Entwickelung zu begreifen, war das unsterbliche Verdienst der von Mannern wie Savigny, Eichhorn und Jacob Grimm gefuhrten historischen Rechtsschule.—GIERKE, *Rundschau*, xviii. 205.

[77] The only effective way of studying what is called the philosophy of religion, or the philosophical criticism of religion, is to study the history of religion. The true science of war is the history of war, the true science of religion is, I believe, the history of religion. —M. MULLER, *Theosophy*, 3, 4. La théologie ne doit plus être que l'histoire des efforts spontanés tentés pour résoudre le problème divin. L'histoire, en effet, est la forme nécessaire de la science de tout ce qui est soumis aux lois de la vie changeante et successive. La science de l'esprit humain, c'est de même, l'histoire de l'esprit humain.—RENAN, *Averroes*, Pref. vi.

[78] Political economy is not a science, in any strict sense, but a body of systematic knowledge gathered

from the study of common processes, which have
been practised all down the history of the human
race in the production and distribution of wealth.—
BONAMY PRICE, *Social Science Congress*, 1878. Such
a study is in harmony with the best intellectual
tendencies of our age, which is, more than anything
else, characterized by the universal supremacy of the
historical spirit. To such a degree has this spirit
permeated all our modes of thinking, that with respect
to every branch of knowledge, no less than with
respect to every institution and every form of human
activity, we almost instinctively ask, not merely what
is its existing condition, but what were its earliest
discoverable germs, and what has been the course
of its development.—INGRAM, *History of Political
Economy*, 2. Wir dagegen stehen keinenAugenblick an,
die Nationalokonomie fur eine reine Erfahrungswis-
senschaft zu erklaren, und die Geschichte ist uns
daher nicht Hulfsmittel, sondern Gegenstand selber —
ROSCHER, *Deutsche Vierteljahrschrift*, 1849, 1. 182.
Der bei weitem grosste Theil menschlicher Irrthumer
beruhet darauf, dass man zeitlich und ortlich Wahres
oder Heilsames fur absolut wahr oder heilsam aus-
giebt. Fur jede Stufe der Volksentwickelung passt
eine besondere Staatsverfassung, die mit allen ubrigen
Verhaltnissen des Volks als Ursache und Wirkung auf's
Innigste verbunden ist ; so passt auch fur jede
Entwickelungsstufe eine besondere Landwirthschafts-
verfassung.—ROSCHER, *Archiv f p. Oek.*, VIII , 2 Heft
1845. Seitdem vor allen Roscher, Hildebrand und
Knies den Werth, die Berechtigung und die Nothwen-

dıgkeıt derselben unwıderleglıch dargethan, hat sıch
immer allgemeiner der Gedanke Bahn gebrochen
dass dıese Wıssenschaft, dıe bis dahin nur auf die
Gegenwart, auf dıe Erkenntnıss der bestehenden
Verhaltnısse und dıe ın ıhnen sıchtbaren Gesetze den
Blıck gerichtet hatte, auch ın die Vergangenheıt, in dıe
Erforschung der bereits hınter uns lıegenden wirthschaft-
lıchen Entwıcklung der Volker sıch vertıefen musse.—
SCHONBERG, *Jahrbucher f. Nationalokonomie und Sta-
tistik*, Neue Folge, 1867, ı. ı.   Schmoller, moins dogmatique et mettant comme une sorte de coquetterıe à
être incertaın, démontre, par les faıts, la fausseté ou
l'arbıtraıre de tous ces postulats, et laisse l'économıe
polıtıque se dıssoudre dans l'hıstoire.—BRETON, *R. de
Parıs*, ıx. 67.   Wer die polıtische Oekonomıe Feuer-
lands unter dieselben Gesetze brıngen wollte mit der
des heutıgen Englands, wurde damıt augenscheınlıch
nıchts zu Tage fordern als den allerbanalsten Gemein-
platz.   Dıe polıtısche Oekonomie ıst somit wesentlıch
eıne hıstorısche Wıssenschaft.   Sıe behandelt einen
geschıchtlichen, das heisst eınen stets wechselnden
Stoff.   Sıe untersucht zunachst dıe besondern Gesetze
jeder eınzelnen Entwicklungsstufe der Produktıon und
des Austausches, und wird erst am Schluss dıeser
Unteısuchung dıe wenigen, fur Produktıon und
Austausch uberhaupt geltenden, ganz allgemeinen
Gesetze aufstellen konnen. — ENGELS, *Duhrings
Umwalzung der Wıssenschaft*, 1878, **121.**

[79] Hıstory preserves the student from beıng led
astray by a too servıle adherence to any system.—
WOLOWSKI.   No system can be anything more than a

history, not in the order of impression, but in the order
of arrangement by analogy.—DAVY, *Memoirs*, 68.
Avec des matériaux si nombreux et si importants, il
fallait bien du courage pour résister à la tentation de
faire un système. De Saussure eut ce courage, et
nous en ferons le dernier trait et le trait principal de
son éloge.—CUVIER, *Éloge de Saussure*, 1810.

[80] C'était, en 1804, une idée heureuse et nouvelle,
d'appeler l'histoire au secours de la science, d'interroger les deux grandes écoles rivales au profit de
la vérité —COUSIN, *Fragments Littéraires*, 1843, 95,
on Dégerando. No branch of philosophical doctrine,
indeed, can be fairly investigated or apprehended
apart from its history. All our systems of politics,
morals, and metaphysics would be different if we knew
exactly how they grew up, and what transformations
they have undergone ; if we knew, in short, the true
history of human ideas.—CLIFFE LESLIE, *Essays in
Political and Moral Philosophy*, 1879, 149. The
history of philosophy must be rational and philosophic
It must be philosophy itself, with all its elements, in
all their relations, and under all their laws represented
in striking characters by the hands of time and of history, in the manifested progress of the human mind.—
SIR WILLIAM HAMILTON, *Edin. Rev.* l. 200, 1829.
Il n'est point d'étude plus instructive, plus utile que
l'étude de l'histoire de la philosophie ; car on y
apprend à se désabuser des philosophes, et l'on y dés-
apprend la fausse science de leurs systèmes.—ROYER
COLLARD, *Œuvres de Reid*, iv. 426. On ne peut
guère échapper à la conviction que toutes les solutions

des questions philosophiques n'aient été développées ou indiquées avant le commencement du dix-neuvième siècle, et que par conséquent il ne soit très difficile, pour ne pas dire impossible, de tomber, en pareille matière, sur une idée neuve de quelque importance. Or si cette conviction est fondée, il s'ensuit que la science est faite.—JOUFFROY, in DAMIRON, *Philosophie du XIXe Siècle*, 363 Le but dernier de tous mes efforts, l'âme de mes écrits et de tout mon enseignement, c'est l'identité de la philosophie et de son histoire.—COUSIN, *Cours de* 1829. Ma route est historique, il est vrai, mais mon but est dogmatique ; je tends à une théorie, et cette théorie je la demande à l'histoire.—COUSIN, *Ph. du XVIIIe Siècle*, 15. L'histoire de la philosophie est contrainte d'emprunter d'abord à la philosophie la lumière qu'elle doit lui rendre un jour avec usure.—COUSIN, *Du Vrai*, 1855, 14. M. Cousin, durant tout son professorat de 1816 à 1829, a pensé que l'histoire de la philosophie était la source de la philosophie même. Nous ne croyons pas exagérer en lui prêtant cette opinion.—B. ST. HILAIRE, *Victor Cousin*, i. 302. Il se hâta de convertir le fait en loi, et proclama que la philosophie, étant identique à son histoire, ne pouvait avoir une loi différente, et était vouée à jamais à l'évolution fatale des quatre systèmes, se contredisant toujours, mais se limitant, et se modérant, par cela même de manière à maintenir l'équilibre, sinon l'harmonie de la pensée humaine.—VACHEROT, *Revue des Deux Mondes*, 1868, iii. 957. Er hat uberhaupt das unvergangliche Verdienst, zuerst in Frankreich zu der Erkenntniss gelangt zu sein, dass die menschliche Vernunft nur durch das

Studium des Gesetzes ihrer Entwickelungen begriff-
en werden kann.—LAUSER, *Unsere Zeit*, 1868, 1
459. Le philosophe en quête du vrai en soi.
n'est plus réduit à ses conceptions individuelles ,
il est riche du trésor amassé par l'humanité.—
BOUTROUX, *Revue Politique*, xxxvii. 802. L'histoire,
je veux dire l'histoire de l'esprit humain, est en
ce sens la vraie philosophie de notre temps.—
RENAN, *Études de Morale*, 83. Die Philosophie wurde
eine hochst bedeutende Hulfswissenschaft der Geschichte, sie hat ihre Richtung auf das Allgemeine gefor-
dert, ihren Blick für dasselbe gescharft, und sie, wenigstens durch ihre Vermittlung, mit Gesichtspuncten,
Ideen, bereichert die sie aus ihrem eigenen Schoosse
sobald noch nicht erzeugt haben wurde Weit die
fruchtbarste darunter war die aus der Naturwissenschaft
geschopfte Idee des organischen Lebens, dieselbe auf
der die neueste Philosophie selbst beruht Die seit zwei
bis drei Jahrzehnten in der Behandlung der Geschichte
eingetretene durchgreifende Veranderung, wie 'die
vollige Umgestaltung so mancher anderen Wissenschaft
. . ist der Hauptsache nach ihr Werk.—HAUG, *Allgemeine Geschichte*, 1841, i. 22 Eine Geschichte der Philosophie in eigentlichen Sinne wurde erst moglich als
man an die Stelle der Philosophen deren Systeme
setzte, den inneren Zusammenhang zwischen diesen
feststellte und — wie Dilthey sagt — mitten in
Wechsel der Philosophien ein siegreiches Fortschreiten zur Wahrheit nachwies. Die Gesammtheit
der Philosophie stellt sich also dar als eine geschichtliche Einheit.—SAUL, *Rundschau*, Feb. 1894, 307.

K

Warum die Philosophie eine Geschichte habe und
haben musse, blieb unerortert, ja ungeahnt, dass die
Philosophie am meisten von allen Wissenschaften
historisch sei, denn man hatte in der Geschichte den
Begriff der Entwicklung nicht entdeckt —MARBACH,
Griechische Philosophie, 15   Was bei oberflachlicher
Betrachtung nur ein Gewirre einzelner Personen und
Meinungen zu sein schien, zeigt sich bei genauerer
und grundlicherer Untersuchung als eine geschichtliche Entwicklung, in der alles, bald naher, bald
entfernter, mit allem anderen zusammenhangt.—
ZELLER, *Rundschau*, Feb 1894, 307. Nur die
Philosophie, die an die geschichtliche Entwickelung
anknupft kann auf bleibenden Erfolg auch fur die
Zukunft rechnen und fortschreiten zu dem, was in der
bisherigen philosophischen Entwickelung nur erst
unvollkommen erreicht oder angestrebt worden ist.
Kann sich doch die Philosophie uberhaupt und
insbesondere die Metaphysik ihrer eigenen geschichtlichen Entwickelung nicht entschlagen, sondern hat
eine Geschichte der Philosophie als eigene und zwar
zugleich historische und spekulative Disziplin, in deren
geschichtlichen Entwickelungsphasen und geschicht-
lich aufeinanderfolgenden Systemen der Philosophen
die neuere Spekulation seit Schelling and Hegel zugleich die Philosophie selbst als ein die verschiedenen
geschichtlichen Systeme umfassendes ganzes in seiner
dialektischen Gliederung erkannt hat.—GLOATZ,
Spekulative Theologie, i 23   Die heutige Philosophie
fuhrt uns auf einen Standpunkt von dem aus die
philosophische Idee als das innere Wesen der Ge-

schichte selbst erscheint. So trat an die Stelle einer abstrakt philosophischen Richtung, welche das Geschichtliche verneinte, eine abstrakt geschichtliche Richtung welche das Philosophische verlaugnete. Beide Richtungen sind als uberschrittene und besiegte zu betrachten —BERNER, *Strafrecht,* 75 Die Geschichte der Philosophie hat uns fast schon die Wissenschaft der Philosophie selbst ersetzt.—HERMANN, *Phil Monatshefte,* ii. 198, 1889

[81] Le siècle actuel sera principalement caractérisé par l'irrévocable prépondérance de l'histoire, en philosophie, en politique, et même en poésie —COMTE, *Politique Positive,* iii. 1.

[82] The historical or comparative method has revolutionized not only the sciences of law, mythology, and language, of anthropology and sociology, but it has forced its way even into the domain of philosophy and natural science. For what is the theory of evolution itself, with all its far-reaching consequences, but the achievement of the historical method ?— PROTHERO, *Inaugural National Review, Dec* 1894, 461. To facilitate the advancement of all the branches of useful science, two things seem to be principally requisite. The first is, an historical account of their rise, progress, and present state. Without the former of these helps, a person every way qualified for extending the bounds of science labours under great disadvantages , wanting the lights which have been struck out by others, and perpetually running the risk of losing his labour, and finding himself anticipated —PRIESTLEY, *History of Vision,* 1772,

1. Pref. 1. Cuvier se proposait de montrer l'enchaînement scientifique des découvertes, leurs relations avec les grands évènements historiques, et leur influence sur les progrès et le développement de la civilisation —DARESTE, *Biographie Générale*, xii. 685. Dans ses éloquentes leçons, l'histoire des sciences est devenue l'histoire même de l'esprit humain ; car, remontant aux causes de leurs progrès et de leurs erreurs, c'est toujours dans les bonnes ou mauvaises routes suivies par l'esprit humain, qu'il trouve ces causes —FLOURENS, *Éloge de Cuvier*, xxxi   Wie keine fortlaufende Entwickelungsreihe von nur Einem Punkte aus vollkommen aufzufassen ist, so wird auch keine lebendige Wissenschaft nur aus der Gegenwart begriffen werden konnen.—Deswegen ist aber eine solche Darstellung doch noch nicht der gesammten Wissenschaft adaquat, und sie birgt, wenn sie damit verwechselt wird, starke Gefahren der Einseitigkeit, des Dogmatismus und damit der Stagnation in sich. Diesen Gefahren kann wirksam nur begegnet werden durch die verstandige Betrachtung der Geschichte der Wissenschaften, welche diese selbst in stetem Flusse zeigt und die Tendenz ihres Fortschreitens in offenbarer und sicherer Weise klarlegt.—ROSENBERGER, *Geschichte der Physik*, iii., p. vi.   Die Continuitat in der Ausbildung aller Auffassungen tritt um so deutlicher hervor, je vollstandiger man sich damit, wie sie zu verschiedenen Zeiten waren, vertraut macht —KOPP, *Entwickelung der Chemie*, 814.

[88] Die Geschichte und die Politik sind Ein und derselbe Janus mit dem Doppelgesicht, das in der

Geschichte in die Vergangenheit, in der Politik in die
Zukunft hinschaut —GUGLER'S *Leben*, ii. 59

[84] The papers inclosed, which give an account of
the killing of two men in the county of Londonderry ;
if they prove to be Tories, 'tis very well they are gone
—I think it will not only be necessary to grant those a
pardon who killed them, but also that they have some
reward for their own and others' encouragement.—
ESSEX, *Letters*, 10, *Jan.* 10, 1675.   The author of
this happened to be present   There was a meeting
of some honest people in the city, upon the occasion
of the discovery of some attempt to stifle the evidence
of the witnesses —Bedloe said he had letters from
Ireland, that there were some Tories to be brought
over hither, who were privately to murder Dr Oates
and the said Bedloe.   The doctor, whose zeal was
very hot, could never after this hear any man talk
against the plot, or against the witnesses, but he
thought he was one of these Tories, and called almost
every man a Tory that opposed him in discourse , till
at last the word Tory became popular —DEFOE,
Edinburgh Review, l 403.

[85] La España será el primer pueblo en donde se
encenderá esta guerra patriotica que solo puede
libertar á Europa.—Hemos oido esto en Inglaterra á
varios de los que estaban alli presentes.   Muchas
veces ha oido lo mismo al duque de Wellington el
general Don Miguel de Alava, y dicho duque refirió
el suceso en una comida diplomatica que dió en Paris
el duque de Richelieu en 1816 —TORENO, *Historia
del Levantamiento de España*, 1838, i. 508.

[86] Nunquam propter auctoritatem illorum, quamvis magni sint nominis (supponimus scilicet semper nos cum eo agere qui scientiam historicam vult consequi), sententias quas secuti sunt ipse tamquam certas admittet, sed solummodo ob vim testimoniorum et argumentorum quibus eas confirmarunt.—DE SMEDT, *Introductio ad historiam critice tractandam*, 1866, 1. 5.

[87] Hundert schwere Verbrechen wiegen nicht so schwer in der Schale der Unsittlichkeit, als ein unsittliches Princip.—*Hallische Jahrbucher*, 1839, 308. Il faut flétrir les crimes, mais il faut aussi, et surtout, flétrir les doctrines et les systèmes qui tendent à les justifier.—MORTIMER TERNAUX, *Histoire de la Terreur*.

[88] We see how good and evil mingle in the best of men and in the best of causes, we learn to see with patience the men whom we like best often in the wrong, and the repulsive men often in the right, we learn to bear with patience the knowledge that the cause which we love best has suffered, from the awkwardness of its defenders, so great disparagement, as in strict equity to justify the men who were assaulting it.—STUBBS, *Seventeen Lectures*, 97.

[89] Caeteris paribus, on trouvera tousjours que ceux qui ont plus de puissance sont sujets à pécher davantage, et il n'y a point de théorème de géométrie qui soit plus asseuré que cette proposition.—LEIBNIZ, 1688, ed. Rommel, II. 197. Il y a toujours eu de la malignité dans la grandeur, et de l'opposition à l'esprit de l'Évangile, mais maintenant il y en a plus que jamais, et il semble que comme le monde va à sa fin,

celui qui est dans l'élévation fait tous ses efforts pour
dominer avec plus de tyrannie, et pour étouffer les
maximes du Christianisme et le règne de Jésus-Christ,
voiant qu'il s'approche. — GODEAU, *Lettres*, 423,
March 27, 1667. There is, in fact, an unconquerable
tendency in all power, save that of knowledge, acting
by and through knowledge, to injure the mind of him
by whom that power is exercised.—WORDSWORTH,
June 22, 1817. *Letters of Lake Poets*, 369.

[90] I cieli han messo sulla terra due giudici delle
umane azioni, la coscienza e la storia.—COLLETTA.
Wenn gerade die edelsten Manner um des Nachruhmes
willen gearbeitet haben, so soll die Geschichte ihre
Belohnung sein, sie auch die Strafe fur die Schlechten
—LASAULX, *Philosophie der Kunste*, 211. Pour juger
ce qui est bon et juste dans la vie actuelle ou passée,
il faut posséder un criterium, qui ne soit pas tiré du
passé ou du présent, mais de la nature humaine.—
AHRENS, *Cours de Droit Naturel*, i. 67.

[91] L'homme de notre temps ! La conscience
moderne ! Voilà encore de ces termes qui nous
ramènent la prétendue philosophie de l'histoire et la
doctrine du progrès, quand il s'agit de la justice, c'est-
à-dire de la conscience pure et de l'homme rationnel,
que d'autres siècles encore que le nôtre ont connu.—
RENOUVIER, *Crit. Phil.* 1873, ii. 55.

[92] Il faut pardonner aux grands hommes le marche-
pied de leur grandeur.—COUSIN, in J. SIMON, *Nos
Hommes d'État*, 1887, 55. L'esprit du XVIIIᵉ siècle
n'a pas besoin d'apologie . l'apologie d'un siècle est
dans son existence.—COUSIN, *Fragments*, iii. 1826.

Suspendus aux lèvres éloquentes de M. Cousin, nous
l'entendîmes s'écrier que la meilleure cause l'emportait
toujours, que c'était la loi de l'histoire, le rhythme
immuable du progrès.—GASPARIN, *La Liberté Morale*,
ii. 63. Cousin verurtheilen heisst darum nichts
Anderes als jenen Geist historischer Betrachtung
verdammen, durch welchen das 19 Jahrhundert die
revolutionare Kritik des 18 Jahrhunderts erganzt,
durch welchen insbesondere Deutschland die geistigen
Wohlthaten vergolten hat, welche es im Zeitalter der
Aufklarung von seinen westlichen Nachbarn empfan-
gen.—IODL, *Gesch der Ethik*, ii 295   Der Gang der
Weltgeschichte steht ausserhalb der Tugend, des
Lasters, und der Gerechtigkeit.—HEGEL, *Werke*, viii
425. Die Vermischung des Zufalligen im Indivi-
duum mit dem an ihm Historischen fuhrt zu
unzahligen falschen Ansichten und Urtheilen. Hierzu
gehort namentlich alles Absprechen uber die moralische
Tuchtigkeit der Individuen, und die Verwunderung,
welche bis zur Verzweiflung an gottlicher Gerechtigkeit
sich steigert, dass historisch grosse Individuen
moralisch nichtswurdig erscheinen konnen   Die
moralische Tuchtigkeit besteht in der Unterordnung
alles dessen was zufallig am Einzelnen unter das an
ihm dem Allgemeinen Angehorige. — MARBACH,
Geschichte der Griechischen Philosophie, 7. Das Sittliche
der Neuseelander, der Mexikaner ist vielmehr ebenso
sittlich, wie das der Griechen, der Romer , und das
Sittliche der Christen des Mittelalters ist ebenso
sittlich, wie das der Gegenwart. — KIRCHMANN,
Grundbegriffe des Rechts, 194. Die Geschichtswissen-

schaft als solche kennt nur ein zeitliches und mithin auch nur ein relatives Maass der Dinge. Alle Werth-beurtheilung der Geschichte kann daher nur relativ und aus zeitlichen Momenten fliessen, und wer sich nicht selbst tauschen und den Dingen nicht Gewalt anthun will, muss ein für allemal in dieser Wissen-schaft auf absolute Werthe verzichten.—LORENZ, *Schlosser*, 80. Only according to his faith is each man judged   Committed as this deed has been by a pure-minded, pious youth, it is a beautiful sign of the time. —DE WETTE to Sand's Mother, CHEYNE, *Founders of Criticism*, 44. The men of each age must be judged by the ideal of their own age and country, and not by the ideal of ours —LECKY, *Value of History*, 50.

[93] La durée ici-bas, c'est le droit, c'est la sanction de Dieu.—GUIRAUD, *Philosophie Catholique de l'Histoire.*

[94] Ceux qui ne sont pas contens de l'ordre des choses ne sçauroient se vanter d'aimer Dieu comme il faut.—Il faut toujours estre content de l'ordre du passé, parce qu'il est conforme à la volonté de Dieu absolue, qu'on connoit par l'évènement. Il faut tâcher de rendre l'avenir, autant qu'il dépend de nous, conforme à la volonté de Dieu présomptive.—LEIBNIZ, *Werke*, ed. Gerhardt, II. 136. Ich habe damals be-kannt und bekenne jetzt, dass die politische Wahrheit aus denselben Quellen zu schopfen ist, wie alle anderen, aus dem gottlichen Willen und dessen Kundgebung in der Geschichte des Menschengeschlechts.—RADO-WITZ, *Neue Gesprache*, 65.

[95] A man is great as he contends best with the circumstances of his age.—FROUDE, *Short Studies* 1.

388. La persuasion que l'homme est avant tout une personne morale et libre, et qu'ayant conçu seul, dans sa conscience et devant Dieu, la règle de sa conduite, il doit s'employer tout entier à l'appliquer en lui, hors de lui, absolument, obstinément, inflexiblement, par une résistance perpétuelle opposée aux autres ; et par une contrainte perpétuelle exercée sur soi, voilà la grande idée anglaise.—TAINE, SOREL, *Discours de Réception*, 24. In jeder Zeit des Christenthums hat es einzelne Manner gegeben, die uber ihrer Zeit standen und von ihren Gegensatzen nicht beruhrt wurden —BACHMANN, *Hengstenberg*, 1. 160. Eorum enim qui de iisdem rebus mecum aliquid ediderunt, aut solus insanio ego, aut solus non insanio, tertium enim non est, nisi (quod dicet forte aliquis) insaniamus omnes —HOBBES, quoted by DE MORGAN, June 3, 1858, *Life of Sir W R Hamilton*, iii 552.

[96] I have now to exhibit a rare combination of good qualities, and a steady perseverance in good conduct, which raised an individual to be an object of admiration and love to all his contemporaries, and have made him to be regarded by succeeding generations as a model of public and private virtue.—The evidence shows that upon this occasion he was not only under the influence of the most vulgar credulity, but that he violated the plainest rules of justice, and that he really was the murderer of two innocent women. —Hale's motives were most laudable —CAMPBELL'S *Lives of the Chief Justices*, 1. 512, 561, 566. It was not to be expected of the colonists of New England that they should be the first to see through a delusion

which befooled the whole civilized world, and the gravest and most knowing persons in it.—The people of New England believed what the wisest men of the world believed at the end of the seventeenth century. —PALFREY, *New England*, IV. 127, 129 (also speaking of witchcraft). Il est donc bien étrange que sa sévérité tardive s'exerce aujourd'hui sur un homme auquel elle n'a d'autre reproche à faire que d'avoir trop bien servi l'état par des mesures politiques, injustes peut-être, violentes, mais qui, en aucune manière, n'avaient l'intérêt personnel du coupable pour objet.—M. Hastings peut sans doute paraître répréhensible aux yeux des étrangers, des particuliers même, mais il est assez extraordinaire qu'une nation usurpatrice d'une partie de l'Indostan veuille mêler les règles de la morale à celles d'une administration forcée, injuste et violente par essence, et à laquelle il faudrait renoncer à jamais pour être conséquent.— MALLET DU PAN, *Memories*, ed. Sayous, I. 102.

[97] On parle volontiers de la stabilité de la constitution anglaise. La vérité est que cette constitution est toujours en mouvement et en oscillation et qu'elle se prête merveilleusement au jeu de ses différentes parties. Sa solidité vient de sa souplesse , elle plie et ne rompt pas.—BOUTMY, *Nouvelle Revue*, 1878, 49.

[98] This is not an age for a man to follow the strict morality of better times, yet sure mankind is not yet so debased but that there will ever be found some few men who will scorn to join concert with the public voice when it is not well grounded.—*Savile Correspondence*, 173.

⁹⁹ Cette proposition L'homme est incomparablement plus porté au mal qu'au bien, et il se fait dans
le monde incomparablement plus de mauvaises actions
que de bonnes —est aussi certaine qu'aucun principe de
métaphysique. Il est donc incomparablement plus
probable qu'une action faite par un homme, est
mauvaise, qu'il n'est probable qu'elle soit bonne.
Il est incomparablement plus probable que ces
secrets ressorts qui l'ont produite sont cor-
rompus, qu'il n'est probable qu'ils soient honnêtes
Je vous avertis que je parle d'une action qui n'est
point mauvaise extérieurement —BAYLE, *Œuvres*,
ii. 248.

¹⁰⁰ A Christian is bound by his very creed to suspect evil, and cannot release himself —His religion
has brought evil to light in a way in which it never
was before , it has shown its depth, subtlety, ubiquity ,
and a revelation, full of mercy on the one hand, is
terrible in its exposure of the world's real state on the
other. The Gospel fastens the sense of evil upon the
mind , a Christian is enlightened, hardened, sharpened,
as to evil , he sees it where others do not.—MOZLEY,
Essays, i 308. All satirists, of course, work in the
direction of Christian doctrine, by the support they
give to the doctrine of original sin, making a sort of
meanness and badness a law of society.—MOZLEY,
Letters, 333. Les critiques, même malveillants, sont
plus près de la vérité dernière que les admirateurs.—
NISARD, *Lit. fr* , Conclusion Les hommes supérieurs
doivent nécessairement passer pour méchants. Où
les autres ne voient ni un défaut, ni un ridicule,

ni un vice, leur implacable œil l'aperçoit.—BARBEY
D'AUREVILLY, *Figaro*, March 31, 1888.

[101] Prenons garde de ne pas trop expliquer, pour
ne pas fournir des arguments à ceux qui veulent tout
excuser.—BROGLIE, *Réception de Sorel*, 46.

[102] The eternal truths and rights of things exist,
fortunately, independent of our thoughts or wishes,
fixed as mathematics, inherent in the nature of man
and the world. They are no more to be trifled
with than gravitation.—FROUDE, *Inaugural Lecture at
St. Andrews*, 1869, 41. What have men to do with
interests? There is a right way and a wrong way.
That is all we need think about.—CARLYLE to
FROUDE, *Longman's Magazine*, Dec 1892, 151. As
to History, it is full of indirect but very effective
moral teaching. It is not only, as Bolingbroke called
it, "Philosophy teaching by examples," but it is
morality teaching by examples.—It is essentially the
study which best helps the student to conceive large
thoughts.—It is impossible to overvalue the moral
teaching of History —FITCH, *Lectures on Teaching*,
432. Judging from the past history of our race, in
ninety-nine cases out of a hundred, war is a folly and
a crime.—Where it is so, it is the saddest and the
wildest of all follies, and the most heinous of all
crimes.—GREG, *Essays on Political and Social Science*,
1853, i. 562. La volonté de tout un peuple ne peut
rendre juste ce qui est injuste les représentants
d'une nation n'ont pas le droit de faire ce que la
nation n'a pas le droit de faire elle-même.—B.
CONSTANT, *Principes de Politique*, i. 15.

[103] Think not that morality is ambulatory, that vices in one age are not vices in another, or that virtues, which are under the everlasting seal of right reason, may be stamped by opinion —SIR THOMAS BROWNE, *Works*, IV. 64

[104] Osons croire qu'il seroit plus à propos de mettre de côté ces traditions, ces usages, et ces coutumes souvent si imparfaites, si contradictoires, si incohérentes, ou de ne les consulter que pour saisir les inconvéniens et les éviter, et qu'il faudroit chercher non-seulement les éléments d'une nouvelle législation, mais même ses derniers détails dans une étude approfondie de la morale.—LETROSNE, *Réflexions sur la Législation Criminelle*, 137. M. Renan appartient à cette famille d'esprits qui ne croient pas en réalité la raison, la conscience, le droit applicables à la direction des sociétés humaines, et qui demandent à l'histoire, à la tradition, non à la morale, les règles de la politique. Ces esprits sont atteints de la maladie du siècle, le scepticisme moral.—PILLON, *Critique Philosophique*, 1 49.

[105] The subject of modern history is of all others, to my mind, the most interesting, inasmuch as it includes all questions of the deepest interest relating not to human things only, but to divine —ARNOLD, *Modern History*, 311.